Everyman's Poetry

Everyman, I will go with thee,
and be thy guide

Elizabeth Barrett Browning

Selected and edited by COLIN GRAHAM

University of Huddersfield

EVERYMAN

J. M. Dent · London

This edition first published by Everyman Paperbacks in 1998
Selection, Introduction and other critical apparatus
© J. M. Dent 1998

J. M. Dent
Orion Publishing Group
Orion House
5 Upper St Martin's Lane
London WC2H 9EA

Typeset by Deltatype Ltd, Birkenhead, Merseyside
Printed in Great Britain by
The Guernsey Press Co. Ltd, Guernsey, C. I.

British Library Cataloguing-in-Publication Data
is available on request

ISBN 0 460 87894 8

Contents

Note on the Author and Editor

ELIZABETH BARRETT was born on 6 March 1806 at Coxhoe Hall, County Durham, the first of eleven children. When she was three years old the family moved to Hope End, Herefordshire. Her writing career began in earnest at the age of eleven when she began composing *The Battle of Marathon*; at fifteen she had published for the first time in a magazine. At this time she also began to feel the effects of an illness, and possible hypochondria, which was to recur for the rest of her life.

Her next volume of poetry, *An Essay on Mind, with Other Poems*, was published in 1826 with the aid of family money. By this time she had a determination to turn poetry into a career. Her next volumes, *Prometheus Bound* (1833) and *The Seraphim, and Other Poems* (1838), proved to be relatively successful and led to the publication, despite long periods of illness and convalescence, of *Poems* (in two volumes) in 1844. In the following year she received the first of many letters from Robert Browning, whose poetry she had mentioned approvingly in 'Lady Geraldine's Courtship' in *Poems*. In May 1845 Robert Browning made his first visit to Elizabeth Barrett and the two married secretly, against the wishes of Elizabeth's father, on 12 September 1845. One week later they eloped clandestinely to Italy.

Elizabeth Barrett Browning then spent most of the remainder of her life in Italy, punctuated by visits to London. It was during this period that her major poetical works were written: *Casa Guidi Windows* (1851) and her long poem *Aurora Leigh* (1857). Her passionate interest in Italian nationalism, the inspiration for *Casa Guidi Windows*, was also apparent in the last volume published during her lifetime, *Poems Before Congress* (1860).

Elizabeth Barrett Browning died, after a winter of illness, in Florence on 29 June 1861. She was buried in the Protestant cemetery in Florence on 1 July 1861. In 1862 Elizabeth Barrett Browning's *Last Poems*, arranged by Robert Browning, were published.

COLIN GRAHAM is Lecturer in English at the University of Huddersfield. He has written on nineteenth-century poetry, Irish literature and post-colonial theory. He has edited Robert Browning, *Men and Women and Other Poems* (Everyman, 1993) and is currently writing *An Introduction to Irish Studies.*

Chronology of Barrett Browning's Life

Year	Life
1806	Elizabeth Barrett born 6 March at Coxhoe Hall, Durham
1809	Barrett family move to Hope End, Herefordshire
1815	Elizabeth Barrett and her parents in Paris
1817	Begins writing *The Battle of Marathon*
1820	*The Battle of Marathon* printed privately. 'Bro' (her brother Edward) goes to Charterhouse
1821	Her poetry is published in a magazine for the first time (*New Monthly Magazine*)
1822	Returns to Hope End after a stay in Gloucester
1823	Holiday in France
1825	Stays with her grandmother in Hastings
1826	*An Essay on Mind, with Other Poems* published (25 March)
1827	Begins her correspondence with Hugh Stuart Boyd
1828	Mary Moulton-Barrett, Elizabeth's mother, dies on 7 October
1830	Death of her paternal grandmother
1831	Keeps a diary during this year
1832	Hope End, the family home, is sold; the Barrett's move to Sidmouth in Devon

Chronology of her Times

Year	Literary Context	Historical Events
1806		Grenville takes over as Prime Minister from Pitt
1807	Wordsworth, *Poems in Two Volumes*	
1809	Tennyson born	Beginning of commercial boom
1812	Dickens born Robert Browning born	Napoleon enters Russia. America declares war on Britain
1813	Jane Austen, *Pride and Prejudice*	East India Company abolished
1814	Wordsworth, *The Excursion*	
1817	Death of Jane Austen	Economic slump follows boom of previous two years
1818	Keats, *Endymion*	
1820	Shelley, *Prometheus Unbound*	Accession of George IV
1821	Death of Keats	
1822	Matthew Arnold born Death of Shelley	Famine in Ireland
1824	Death of Byron	
1825		Trades unions legalised
1827	Clare, *The Shepherd's Calendar*	
1829		Catholic emancipation
1830	Tennyson, *Poems, Chiefly Lyrical*	Accession of William IV. Revolutions in Europe
1832	Death of Walter Scott	First Reform Act

Year	Life
1833	*Prometheus Unbound* published
1835	Barrett family move to London
1838	*The Seraphim, and Other Poems* published. Elizabeth goes to Torquay for a period of convalescence
1840	Edward Moulton-Barrett, Elizabeth's brother, drowns
1841	Returns to London
1844	*Poems* (2 volumes) published
1845	In January Robert Browning writes his first letter to Elizabeth Barrett. Visits her first in May
1846	Elizabeth Barrett and Robert Browning marry secretly on 12 September. They leave clandestinely for Italy one week later
1847	Brownings live in Pisa, then Florence
1848	Begins writing *Casa Guidi Windows*
1849	Birth of Elizabeth's son 'Pen' (Robert Weidemann Browning)
1850	New edition of *Poems* is published
1851	The Brownings return to London for the first time since their elopement. *Casa Guidi Windows* published
1852	Visits London again, staying at Paris on the return journey to Florence
1853	Begins writing *Aurora Leigh*
1854	Returns to Florence after travels around Italy
1855	After an illness early in the year, visits London
1856	*Aurora Leigh* completed
1857	Death of Edward Barrett Moulton-Barrett, Elizabeth's father. *Aurora Leigh* published
1858	Holidays in France

Year	Literary Context	Historical Events
1833	Carlyle, *Sartor Resartus*	Abolition of slavery in British Empire
1837	Dickens, *Oliver Twist*	Accession of Victoria
1838	Dickens, *Nicholas Nickleby*	Anti-Corn Law League established
1841	Robert Browning, *Pippa Passes*	
1842	Tennyson, *Poems*	Chartist riots
1843	Death of Southey Wordsworth becomes Poet Laureate	
1846		Corn Law abolished
1847	Charlotte Brontë, *Jane Eyre*	
1848	Thackeray, *Vanity Fair*	Revolutions in Europe
1850	Death of Wordworth	
1851	Ruskin, *Stones of Venice*	Great Exhibition
1853	Matthew Arnold, *Poems*	
1854	Dickens, *Hard Times*	Crimean War begins
1855	Robert Browning, *Men and Women*	
1856	Thomas Hughes, *Tom Brown's Schooldays*	Treaty of Paris
1857	Trollope, *Barchester Towers*	Indian Mutiny

Year	Life
1859	Returns to Florence from Rome. Illness
1860	*Poems Before Congress* published. Death of her sister Henrietta
1861	Winter brings on illness while in Rome. Returns to Florence in June. Death of Elizabeth Barrett Browning on 29 June. Buried 1 July in Protestant cemetery in Florence

Year	Literary Context	Historical Events
1859	Darwin, *Origin of the Species*	Construction of Suez Canal begins
1861	J. S. Mill, *Utilitarianism*	Prince Albert dies. Beginning of American Civil War

Introduction

Elizabeth Barrett Browning's reputation has enjoyed mixed fortunes. During her lifetime she was one of the most famous and respected intellectual figures of the Victorian era; she was even very seriously suggested as a possible candidate to be the successor as Poet Laureate to Wordsworth. For most of her life her poetry was better known and more highly regarded than that of her husband, Robert Browning. But after her death, Robert's reputation grew, while Elizabeth was often unfavourably compared to other women poets (most usually Christina Rossetti). The fact that critical accounts of Barrett Browning were framed in these two ways (by comparisons to her husband and to other women) points towards the place from which a renewed interest in her remarkable, often startling poetry would come. It has been historians and critics of women's literature who have, in the later twentieth century, 'rediscovered' the abilities and idiosyncrasies of Barrett Browning, and who have found in her poetry statements and attitudes about women and society which are in some places fascinatingly of their time, and in others profoundly ahead of their time. Reading Barrett Browning as a woman writer is not the only way to think of her work (she was gifted in the crafting and structuring of her verse; she was interested in radicalism, in European politics and in the occult), but it has proved to be an excellent way in which to begin reading Barrett Browning's poetry again.

Elizabeth Barrett's early life (which might even be thought of as the time before she corresponded with Robert Browning in 1845, by which time she was thirty-eight) was dominated by the presences of three men: her father (who tried to prevent her and any of his other children marrying), her brother Edward (known as 'Bro') and Hugh Boyd, a classical scholar who heavily influenced her reading and early intellectual development. Her devotion to these men was intense and they may be seen to represent the emotional and intellectual fetters which were to restrict, or at the very least dominate, her early poetry.

'To My Father on His Birthday', published in *An Essay on Mind*, *with Other Poems* (1826) seems at first sight a reflection of this devotion, written in a classicised poetic form, and through this attempting to gain the recognition of the father. As the quotation from Horace which stands as an epigraph to this poem suggests, 'my father was the reason for these things,' and the poem seems to have a belief in the near-divine inspiration of the paternal.

> No thoughts of fondness e'er appear
> *More* fond, than those I write of here!
> No name can e'er on tablet shine,
> My father! more beloved than *thine!*

Yet the poem may also contain the germ of an uneasiness about the power and role of the father figure in general. The poem is replete with emphatic statements of affection, which, as the poem progresses, tend a little towards hollowness. 'To My Father' ends:

> But still my Father's looks remain
> The best Maecenas of my strain;
> My gentlest joy, upon his brow
> To read the smile, that meets me now –
> To hear him, in his kindness, say
> The words, – perchance he'll speak today!

The final couplet is awkward, reading almost like parody, while stressing the importance of the father's speech and language for the poetry of his daughter. The 'strain' here may have a double edge and it is tempting to read this as a foreshadowing of Aurora Leigh (whose education is consciously set out in her father's as opposed to her mother's 'tongue') discovering her father's library:

> Books! Books! Books!
> I had found the secret of the garret-room
> Piled high with cases in my father's name,
> Piled high, packed large . . .
> (*Aurora Leigh*, First Book (see extracts from
> *Aurora Leigh* below, line 228 ff))

By the time of *Aurora Leigh* Barrett Browning was registering a much more conscious recognition that it is the 'father's name', in the shape of a dominant masculinity, which presides over both knowledge and poetry (commodities Barrett Browning was eager to possess). The encouraging Maecenas who is Moulton-Barrett is, in *Aurora Leigh*, transformed into the sets of secret knowledge hidden from Aurora the poet. Poetry changes from being sanctioned by the father in Barrett Browning's earlier writing, to become an intellectual experience which has to be secretly wrested from closed packing cases, significantly placed in the deliberately poetically clichéd garret-room, and labelled paternally.

Elizabeth Barrett's early life was then deeply affected by this series of relationships with men, all of which were vitally important to her intellectual development, but all of which were also deeply unsatisfactory. Her relationship with the elderly Boyd gave her a knowledge of and almost an awe for classicism (an influence apparent in 'To My Father on His Birthday'), while her affection for 'Bro' was certainly intellectually vital and at times passionate. And her relationships with these men forced a focus on what became a central concern for her poetry later: the problem of the apparent necessity to address her poetry at least partially *to* men. *Aurora Leigh* and *Sonnets from the Portuguese* explore this difficulty, both in terms of poetic form and in their interwoven narratives and contemplations. Negotiating her position as a female poet with these paternal and masculine influences led in two directions; in personal terms, Barrett Browning's reaction was to shut herself off from any event which might earn the 'disapprobation' of her father (until, that is, she met Robert Browning).

In poetic terms, Barrett Browning was faced with the dilemma forced upon the female poet by an apparent lack of satisfactory predecessors and the pressure to write, for the sake of acceptance, in recognised 'male' forms. The method *Sonnets from the Portuguese* employs to overcome these difficulties of audience, influence and the charge of being 'lightweight', is one partially embodied in the dramatic monologue form used by both Robert and Elizabeth Barrett Browning; masks, adopted personae and pretences are used to open new perspectives and at times to call the bluff of standard practices. The *Sonnets* are both deliberately authorless (or authoressless) and *not* 'from the Portuguese', and so are doubly removed from the direct engagement of the female poet with the extended analysis of passion which the *Sonnets* undertake.

Barrett Browning also skilfully employs standard poetic forms (blank verse and, at times, the epic) in *Aurora Leigh*, a poem which addresses its own form and its relationship to 'male' epic forms, and which is written in assured and subtle iambic pentameters, yet which also cuttingly addresses major social issues (rape and prostitution, for example). *Aurora Leigh* is remarkable enough for its narrative abilities, but as feminist critics have hinted at and in places examined, *Aurora Leigh* also involves complexly evolving attempts to create forms of poetic expression apt to the woman poet, forms which are capable of addressing the pressures of masculinity on poetry and the need for any 'difference' in female poetic expression. As an example of this one can take the opening of the 'Fifth Book', with the paragraph beginning:

> Aurora Leigh, be humble. Shall I hope
> To speak my poems in mysterious tune
> With man and nature? – with the lava-lymph . . .

Here the often repeated 'Aurora Leigh, be humble' signals the beginning of a contemplation of the new and the unsettled; this phrase is used constantly in the poem to mark both the extent to which Aurora feels awkward in assuming her role as a thinker and the ability she has to retrace her thoughts and revise what she uncovers. The sentence which follows is one of the most tortuous in the poem, made up of a series of clauses each reformulating and asking a parallel question to 'Shall I hope/ To speak my poems in mysterious tune/ With man and nature?', a set of questions which are then restated in 'can I speak my verse'. The sentence is finally brought to a conclusion at line 445 (in this edition) and like the end of a parenthesis is enclosed by the repeated (though more positively expressed) phrase 'Go,/ Aurora Leigh: be humble.' This grammatical awkwardness and difficulty is no accident. The series of clauses which make up the bulk of the sentence may be grammatically parallel, but they build on each other for specific effects. Take, for example, the lines:

> With spring's delicious trouble in the ground,
> Tormented by the quickened blood of roots,
> And softly pricked by golden crocus sheaves
> In token of the harvest-time of flowers?

The question here is explicitly about the 'mysterious tune' which the female poet must write in; the harmony which she needs to achieve between 'nature' and 'man' (a term used ironically here – is it male or human?). In putting together this fundamental question about whether women's poetry is possible, Aurora begins to show that it is. Standard poetic images of spring are celebratory (both the opening of Chaucer's *The Canterbury Tales* and Wordsworth's 'I wandered lonely as a cloud' are sources here); Aurora's rendition of spring adds a different dimension: 'delicious trouble' appears to be in 'mysterious tune' with nature, so that the regeneration of spring is close to pregnancy and childbirth, involving pain and ecstasy. The notion of spring as regenerative and reproductive, yet close to the feminine, is repeated by images of menstruation in 'Tormented by the quickened blood of roots' and loss of virginity in 'softly pricked by the crocus-sheaves'. This feminised revision of staid poetic imagery culminates in the extraordinary lines:

> . . . with all that strain
> Of sexual passion, which devours the flesh
> In a sacrament of souls? with mother's breasts
> Which, round the new-made creatures hanging there,
> Throb luminous and harmonious like pure spheres?

Here the standard poetic image (the usually metaphysical 'spheres' which represent the universe and its harmonies in totality) is made radically female, a process which the previous revision of spring prepared the reader for. Such is the remarkable detail, care and vigour with which Barrett Browning writes.

Elizabeth Barrett Browning's poetry embodies ideas and energies which exceed the capacities of any single reading. Any reader of Barrett Browning is confronted with a poet who writes (often self-consciously) in an intellectual way, exploring and creating 'neologisms' (as Aurora calls new thinking) within carefully and skilfully crafted verse forms. The combination of poetic technique, energy and ideas becomes an interdependent relationship in her writing, and makes Barrett Browning one of the most challenging and rewarding Victorian poets.

COLIN GRAHAM

Elizabeth Barrett Browning

To My Father on his Birthday

Causa fuit Pater his.
HORACE

Amidst the days of pleasant mirth,
That throw their halo round our earth;
Amidst the tender thoughts that rise
To call bright tears to happy eyes;
Amidst the silken words that move
To syllable the names we love;
There glides no day of gentle bliss
More soothing to the heart than *this*!
No thoughts of fondness e'er appear
More fond, than those I write of here!   10
No name can e'er on tablet shine,
My Father! more beloved than *thine*!
    'Tis sweet, adown the shady past,
A lingering look of love to cast –
Back th' enchanted world to call
That beamed around us first of all;
And walk with Memory fondly o'er
The paths where Hope had been before –
Sweet to receive the sylphic sound
That breathes in tenderness around,   20
Repeating to the listening ear
The names that made our childhood dear –
For parted Joy, like Echo, kind,
Will leave her dulcet voice behind,
To tell, amidst the magic air,
How oft she smiled and lingered there.
Oh! let the deep Aonian shell
Breathe tuneful numbers, clear and well,
While the glad Hours, in fair array,
Lead on this buxom Holiday;   30
And Time, as on his way he springs
Hates the last bard who gave him wings;
For 'neath thy gentleness of praise,

My Father! rose my early lays!
And when the lyre was scarce awake,
I loved its strings for *thy* loved sake;
Wooed the kind Muses – but the while
Thought only how to win thy smile –
My proudest fame – my dearest pride –
More dear than all the world beside!   40
And now, perchance, I seek the tone
For magic that is more its own;
But still my Father's looks remain
The best Maecenas of my strain;
My gentlest joy, upon his brow
To read the smile, that meets me now –
To hear him, in his kindness, say
The words, – perchance he'll speak today!

A Sea-Side Meditation

Ut per aquas quae nunc rerum simulacra videmus.
LUCRETIUS

Go, travel 'mid the hills! The summer's hand
Hath shaken pleasant freshness o'er them all.
Go, travel 'mid the hills! There, tuneful streams
Are touching myriad stops, invisible;
And winds, and leaves, and birds, and your own thoughts
(Not the least glad) in wordless chorus, crowd
Around the thymele of Nature.
                              Go,
And travel onward. Soon shall leaf and bird,
Wind, stream, no longer sound. Thou shalt behold
Only the pathless sky, and houseless sward;   10
O'er which anon are spied innumerous sails
Of fisher vessels like the wings o' the hill,
And white as gulls above them, and as fast,–
But sink they – sink they out of sight. And now
The wind is springing upward in your face;

And, with its fresh-toned gushings, you may hear
Continuous sound which is not of the wind,
Nor of the thunder, nor o' the cataract's
Deep passion, nor o' the earthquake's wilder pulse;
But which rolls on in stern tranquillity,   20
As memories of evil o'er the soul;–
Boweth the bare broad Heaven. – What view you? sea – and
    sea!

The sea – the glorious sea! from side to side
Swinging the grandeur of his foamy strength,
And undersweeping the horizon, – on –
On – with his life and voice inscrutable.
Pause: sit you down in silence! I have read
Of that Athenian, who, when ocean raged,
Unchained the prisoned music of his lips
By shouting to the billows, sound for sound.   30
I marvel how his mind would let his tongue
Affront thereby the ocean's solemnness.
Are we not mute, or speak restrainedly,
When overhead the trampling tempests go,
Dashing their lightning from their hoofs? and when
We stand beside the bier? and when we see
The strong bow down to weep – and stray among
Places which dust or mind hath sanctified?
Yea! for such sights and acts do tear apart
The close and subtle clasping of a chain,   40
Formed not of gold, but of corroded brass,
Whose links are furnished from the common mine
Of every day's event, and want, and wish;
From work-times, diet-times, and sleeping-times:
And thence constructed, mean and heavy links
Within the pandemonic walls of sense
Enchain our deathless part, constrain our strength,
And waste the goodly stature of our soul.
Howbeit, we love this bondage; we do cleave
Unto the sordid and unholy thing,   50
Fearing the sudden wrench required to break
Those clasped links. Behold! all sights and sounds
In air, and sea, and earth, and under earth,

All flesh, all life, all ends, are mysteries;
And all that is mysterious dreadful seems,
And all we cannot understand we fear.
Ourselves do scare ourselves: we hide our sight
In artificial nature from the true,
And throw sensation's veil associative
On God's creation, man's intelligence;   60
Bowing our high imaginings to eat
Dust, like the serpent, once erect as they;
Binding conspicuous on our reason's brow
Phylacteries of shame; learning to feel
By rote, and act by rule (man's rule, not God's!),
Unto our words grow echoes, and our thoughts
A mechanism of spirit.
                    Can this last?
No! not for ay. We cannot subject ay
The heaven-born spirit to the earth-born flesh.
Tame lions *will* scent blood, and appetite   70
Carnivorous glare from out their restless eyes.
Passions, emotions, sudden changes, throw
Our nature back upon us, till we burn.
What warmed Cyrene's fount? As poets sing,
The *change* from light to dark, from dark to light.

All that doth force this nature back on us,
All that doth force the mind to view the mind,
Engend'reth what is named by men, *sublime*.
Thus when, our wonted valley left, we gain
The mountain's horrent brow, and mark from thence   80
The sweep of lands extending with the sky;
Or view the spanless plain; or turn our sight
Upon yon deep's immensity; – we breathe
As if our breath were marble: to and fro
Do reel our pulses, and our words are mute.
We cannot mete by parts, but grapple all;
We cannot measure with our eye, but soul;
And fear is on us. The extent unused,
Our spirit, sends, to spirit's element,
To seize upon abstraction: first on space,   90
The which *eternity in place* I deem;

And then upon eternity; till thought
Hath formed a mirror from their secret sense,
Wherein we view ourselves, and back recoil
At our own awful likeness; ne'ertheless,
Cling to that likeness with a wonder wild,
And while we tremble, glory – proud in fear.
So ends the prose of life: and so shall be
Unlocked her poetry's magnific store.
And so, thou pathless and perpetual sea,   100
So, o'er thy deeps, I brooded and must brood,
Whether I view thee in thy dreadful peace,
Like a spent warrior hanging in the sun
His glittering arms, and meditating death;
Or whether thy wild visage gath'reth shades,
What time thou marshall'st forth thy waves who hold
A covenant of storms, then roar and wind
Under the racking rocks; as martyrs lie
Wheel-bound; and, dying, uter lofty words!
Whether the strength of day is young and high,   110
Or whether, weary of the watch, he sits
Pale on thy wave, and weeps himself to death;–
In storm and calm, at morn and eventide,
Still have I stood beside thee, and out-thrown
My spirit onward on thine element,–
Beyond thine element, – to tremble low
Before those feet which trod thee as they trod
Earth, – to the holy, happy, peopled place,
Where there is no more sea. Yea, and my soul,
Having put on thy vast similitude,   120
Hath wildly moaned at her proper depth,
Echoed her proper musings, veiled in shade
Her secrets of decay, and exercised
An elemental strength, in casting up
Rare gems and things of death on fancy's shore,
Till Nature said 'Enough.'
                Who longest dreams,
Dreams not for ever; seeing day and night
And corporal feebleness divide his dreams,
And on his elevate creations weigh
With hunger, cold, heat, darkness, weariness: 130

Else should we be like gods; else would the course
Of thought's free wheels, increased in speed and might
By an eterne volution, oversweep
The heights of wisdom, and invade her depths:
So, knowing all things, should we have all power;
For is not Knowledge power? But mighty spells
Our operation sear; the Babel must,
Or ere it touch the sky, fall down to earth:
The web, half formed, must tumble from our hands,
And, ere they can resume it, lie decayed.   140
Mind struggles vainly from the flesh. E'en so,
Hell's angel (saith a scroll apocryphal)
Shall, when the latter days of earth have shrunk
Before the blast of God, affect his heaven;
Lift his scarred brow, confirm his rebel heart,
Shoot his strong wings, and darken pole and pole,—
Till day be blotted into night; and shake
The fevered clouds, as if a thousand storms
Throbbed into life! Vain hope – vain strength – vain flight!
God's arm shall meet God's foe, and hurl him back!   150

Man And Nature

A sad man on a summer day
Did look upon the earth and say –

'Purple cloud, the hill-top binding,
Folded hills, the valleys wind in,
Valleys, with fresh streams among you,
Streams, with bosky trees along you,
Trees, with many birds and blossoms,
Birds, with music-trembling bosoms,
Blossoms, dropping dews that wreathe you
To your fellow flowers beneath you,   10
Flowers, that constellate on earth,
Earth, that shakest to the mirth

Of the merry Titan ocean,
All his shining hair in motion!
Why am I thus the only one
Who can be dark beneath the sun?'

But when the summer day was past,
He looked to heaven and smiled at last,
Self-answered so –
                'Because, O cloud,
Pressing with thy crumpled shroud   20
Heavily on mountain top, –
Hills, that almost seem to drop
Stricken with a misty death
To the valleys underneath, –
Valleys, sighing with the torrent, –
Waters, streaked with branches horrent, –
Branchless trees, that shake your head
Wildly o'er your blossoms spread
Where the common flowers are found, –
Flowers, with foreheads to the ground, –   30
Ground, that shriekest while the sea
With his iron smiteth thee –
I am, besides, the only one
Who can be bright *without* the sun.'

De Profundis

1

The face which, duly as the sun,
Rose up for me with life begun,
To mark all bright hours of the day
With hourly love, is dimmed away, –
And yet my days go on, go on.

2

The tongue which, like a stream, could run
Smooth music from the roughest stone,
And every morning with 'Good day'
Make each day good, is hushed away, –
And yet my days go on, go on.   10

3

The heart which, like a staff, was one
For mine to lean and rest upon,
The strongest on the longest day
With steadfast love, is caught away, –
And yet my days go on, go on.

4

And cold before my summer's done,
And deaf in Nature's general tune,
And fallen too low for special fear,
And here, with hope no longer here, –
While the tears drop, my days go on.   20

5

The world goes whispering to its own,
'This anguish pierces to the bone';
And tender friends go sighing round,
'What love can ever cure this wound?'
My days go on, my days go on.

6

The past rolls forward on the sun
And makes all night. O dreams begun,
Not to be ended! Ended bliss,
And life that will not end in this!
My days go on, my days go on.   30

7

Breath freezes on my lips to moan:
As one alone, once not alone,
I sit and knock at Nature's door,

Heart-bare, heart-hungry, very poor,
Whose desolated days go on.

8

I knock and cry, – Undone, undone!
Is there no help, no comfort, – none?
No gleaning in the wide wheat-plains
Where others drive their loaded wains?
My vacant days go on, go on.   40

9

This Nature, though the snows be down,
Thinks kindly of the bird of June:
The little red hip on the tree
Is ripe for such. What is for me,
Whose days so winterly go on?

10

No bird am I, to sing in June,
And dare not ask an equal boon.
Good nests and berries red are Nature's
To give away to better creatures, –
And yet my days go on, go on.   50

11

I ask less kindness to be done, –
Only to loose these pilgrim-shoon
(Too early worn and grimed), with sweet
Cool deathly touch to these tired feet,
Till days go out which now go on.

12

Only to lift the turf unmown
From off the earth where it has grown,
Some cubit-space, and say, 'Behold,
Creep in, poor Heart, beneath that fold,
Forgetting how the days go on.'   60

13

What harm would that do? Green anon
The sward would quicken, overshone

By skies as blue; and crickets might
Have leave to chirp there day and night
While my new rest went on, went on.

14

From gracious Nature have I won
Such liberal bounty? may I run
So, lizard-like, within her side,
And there be safe, who now am tried
By days that painfully go on?   70

15

– A Voice reproves me thereupon,
More sweet than Nature's when the drone
Of bees is sweetest, and more deep
Than when the rivers overleap
The shuddering pines, and thunder on.

16

God's Voice, not Nature's! Night and noon
He sits upon the great white throne
And listens for the creatures' praise.
What babble we of days and days?
The Dayspring He, whose days go on.   80

17

He reigns above, He reigns alone;
Systems burn out and leave His throne:
Fair mists of seraphs melt and fall
Around Him, changeless amid all, –
Ancient of Days, whose days go on.

18

He reigns below, He reigns alone,
And, having life in love forgone
Beneath the crown of sovran thorns,
He reigns the Jealous God. Who mourns
Or rules with Him, while days go on?   90

19

By anguish which made pale the sun,
I hear Him charge His saints that none
Among His creatures anywhere
Blaspheme against Him with despair,
However darkly days go on.

20

Take from my head the thorn-wreath brown!
No mortal grief deserves that crown.
O súpreme Love, chief Misery,
The sharp regalia are for THEE
Whose days eternally go on!   100

21

For us, – whatever's undergone,
Thou knowest, willest what is done.
Grief may be joy misunderstood;
Only the Good discerns the good.
I trust Thee while my days go on.

22

Whatever's lost, if first was won:
We will not struggle nor impugn.
Perhaps the cup was broken here,
That Heaven's new wine might show more clear.
I praise Thee while my days go on.   110

23

I praise Thee while my days go on;
I love Thee while my days go on:
Through dark and dearth, through fire and frost,
With emptied arms and treasure lost,
I thank Thee while my days go on.

24

And having in Thy life-depth thrown
Being and suffering (which are one),
As a child drops his pebble small
Down some deep well, and hears it fall
Smiling – so I. THY DAYS GO ON.   120

Grief

I tell you, hopeless grief is passionless;
That only men incredulous of despair,
Half-taught in anguish, through the midnight air
Beat upward to God's throne in loud access
Of shrieking and reproach. Full desertness
In souls, as countries, lieth silent-bare
Under the blanching, vertical eye-glare
Of the absolute Heavens. Deep-hearted man, express
Grief for thy Dead in silence like to death: –
Most like a monumental statue set   10
In everlasting watch and moveless woe,
Till itself crumble to the dust beneath.
Touch it: the marble eyelids are not wet;
If it could weep, it could arise and go.

Tears

Thank God, bless God, all ye who suffer not
More grief than ye can weep for. That is well –
That is light grieving! lighter, none befell
Since Adam forfeited the primal lot.
Tears! what are tears? The babe weeps in its cot,
The mother singing, – at her marriage-bell
The bride weeps, – and before the oracle
Of high-faned hills, the poet has forgot
Such moisture on his cheeks. Thank God for grace,
Ye who weep only! If, as some have done,   10
Ye grope tear-blinded in a desert place
And touch but tombs, – look up! those tears will run
Soon in long rivers down the lifted face,
And leave the vision clear for stars and sun.

Substitution

When some beloved voice that was to you
Both sound and sweetness, faileth suddenly,
And silence against which you dare not cry,
Aches round you like a strong disease and new –
What hope? what help? what music will undo
That silence to your sense? Not friendship's sigh –
Not reason's subtle count; not melody
Of viols, nor of pipes that Faunus blew.
Not songs of poets, nor of nightingales
Whose hearts leap upward through the cypress-trees   10
To the clear moon! nor yet the spheric laws
Self-chanted, – nor the angels' sweet All hails,
Met in the smile of God: nay, none of these.
Speak THOU, availing Christ! – and fill this pause.

Catarina to Camoëns

DYING IN HIS ABSENCE ABROAD,
AND REFERRING TO THE POEM IN WHICH
HE RECORDED THE SWEETNESS OF
HER EYES

1
On the door you will not enter,
    I have gazed too long – adieu!
Hope withdraws her peradventure –
    Death is near me, – and not *you.*
        Come, O lover,
        Close and cover
These poor eyes, you called, I ween,
'Sweetest eyes, were ever seen.'

2
When I heard you sing that burden
    In my vernal days and bowers,   10

Other praises disregarding,
  But I hearkened that of yours –
    Only saying
    In heart-playing,
'Blessed eyes mine eyes have been,
If the sweetest, HIS have seen!'

3

But all changes. At this vesper,
  Cold the sun shines down the door.
If you stood there, would you whisper
  'Love, I love you,' as before, –   20
    Death pervading
    Now, and shading
Eyes you sang of, that yestreen,
As the sweetest ever seen?

4

Yes, I think, were you beside them,
  Near the bed I die upon, –
Though their beauty you denied them,
  As you stood there, looking down,
    You would truly
    Call them duly,   30
For the love's sake found therein, –
'Sweetest eyes, were ever seen.'

5

And if *you* looked down upon them,
  And if *they* looked up to *you*,
All the light which has foregone them
  Would be gathered back anew.
    They would truly
    Be as duly
Love-transformed to beauty's sheen, –
'Sweetest eyes, were ever seen.'   40

6

But, ah me! you only see me,
  In your thoughts of loving man,

Smiling soft perhaps and dreamy
  Through the wavings of my fan, –
    And unweeting
    Go repeating,
In your reverie serene,
'Sweetest eyes, were ever seen.'

                    7
While my spirit leans and reaches
  From my body still and pale,   50
Fain to hear what tender speech is
  In your love to help my bale –
    O my poet,
    Come and show it!
Come, of latest love, to glean
'Sweetest eyes, were ever seen.'

                    8
O my poet, O my prophet,
  When you praised their sweetness so,
Did you think, in singing of it,
  That it might be near to go?   60
    Had you fancies
    From their glances,
That the grave would quickly screen
'Sweetest eyes, were ever seen'?

                    9
No reply! the fountain's warble
  In the court-yard sounds alone.
As the water to the marble
  So my heart falls with a moan
    From love-sighing
    To this dying.   70
Death forerunneth Love to win
'Sweetest eyes, were ever seen.'

                    10
Will you come? When I'm departed
  Where all sweetnesses are hid;

Where thy voice, my tender-hearted,
  Will not lift up either lid.
    Cry, O lover,
    Love is over!
Cry beneath the cypress green –
'Sweetest eyes, were ever seen.'   80

11

When the angelus is ringing,
  Near the convent will you walk,
And recall the choral singing
  Which brought angels down our talk?
    Spirit-shriven
    I viewed Heaven,
Till you smiled – 'Is earth unclean,
Sweetest eyes, were ever seen?'

12

When beneath the palace-lattice,
  You ride slow as you have done,   90
And you see a face there – that is
  Not the old familiar one, –
    Will you oftly
    Murmur softly,
'Here, ye watched me morn and e'en,
Sweetest eyes, were ever seen'?

13

When the palace-ladies, sitting
  Round your gittern, shall have said,
'Poet, sing those verses written
  For the lady who is dead,'   100
    Will you tremble,
    Yet dissemble, –
Or sing hoarse, with tears between,
'Sweetest eyes, were ever seen'?

14

'Sweetest eyes!' how sweet in flowings
  The repeated cadence is!

Though you sang a hundred poems,
  Still the best one would be this.
    I can hear it
    'Twixt my spirit   110
And the earth-noise intervene –
'Sweetest eyes, were ever seen!'

15

But the priest waits for the praying,
  And the choir are on their knees,
And the soul must pass away in
  Strains more solemn high than these.
    Miserere
    For the weary!
Oh, no longer for Catrine,
'Sweetest eyes, were ever seen!'   120

16

Keep my ribbon, take and keep it
  (I have loosed it from my hair),
Feeling, while you overweep it,
  Not alone in your despair,
    Since with saintly
    Watch unfaintly
Out of heaven shall o'er you lean
'Sweetest eyes, were ever seen.'

17

But – but *now* – yet unremovèd
  Up to Heaven, they glisten fast.   130
You may cast away, Belovèd,
  In your future all my past.
    Such old phrases
    May be praises
For some fairer bosom-queen –
'Sweetest eyes, were ever seen!'

18

Eyes of mine, what are ye doing?
  Faithless, faithless, – praised amiss

If a tear be of your showing,
   Dropt for any hope of HIS!   140
      Death has boldness
      Besides coldness,
If unworthy tears demean
'Sweetest eyes, were ever seen.'

19

I will look out to his future;
   I will bless it till it shine.
Should he ever be a suitor
   Unto sweeter eyes than mine,
      Sunshine gild them,
      Angels shield them,   150
Whatsoever eyes terrene
Be the sweetest HIS have seen!

Flush Or Faunus

You see this dog. It was but yesterday
I mused forgetful of his presence here
Till thought on thought drew downward tear on tear,
When from the pillow where wet-cheeked I lay,
A head as hairy as Faunus thrust its way
Right sudden against my face, – two golden-clear
Great eyes astonished mine, – a drooping ear
Did flap me on either cheek to dry the spray!
I started first as some Arcadian
Amazed by goatly god in twilight grove,   10
But as the bearded vision closelier ran
My tears off, I knew Flush, and rose above
Surprise and sadness, – thanking the true PAN
Who, by low creatures, leads to heights of love.

Hiram Powers' Greek Slave

They say Ideal beauty cannot enter
The house of anguish. On the threshold stands
An alien Image with enshackled hands,
Called the Greek Slave! as if the artist meant her
(That passionless perfection which he lent her,
Shadowed not darkened where the sill expands)
To, so, confront man's crimes in different lands
With man's ideal sense. Pierce to the centre,
Art's fiery finger! – and break up ere long
The serfdom of this world! appeal, fair stone,   10
From God's pure heights of beauty against man's wrong!
Catch up in thy divine face, not alone
East griefs but west, – and strike and shame the strong,
By thunders of white silence, overthrown.

The Runaway Slave at
Pilgrim's Point

1

I stand on the mark beside the shore
   Of the first white pilgrim's bended knee,
Where exile turned to ancestor,
   And God was thanked for liberty.
I have run through the night, my skin is as dark,
I bend my knee down on this mark:
   I look on the sky and the sea.

2

O pilgrim-souls, I speak to you!
   I see you come proud and slow
From the land of the spirits pale as dew   10
   And round me and round me ye go.

O pilgrims, I have gasped and run
All night long from the whips of one
   Who in your names works sin and woe!

3

And thus I thought that I would come
   And kneel here where ye knelt before,
And feel your souls around me hum
   In undertone to the ocean's roar;
And lift my black face, my black hand,
Here, in your names, to curse this land   20
   Ye blessed in freedom's, evermore.

4

I am black, I am black,
   And yet God made me, they say:
But if He did so, smiling back
   He must have cast His work away
Under the feet of His white creatures,
With a look of scorn, that the dusky features
   Might be trodden again to clay.

5

And yet He has made dark things
   To be glad and merry as light: 30
There's a little dark bird sits and sings,
   There's a dark stream ripples out of sight,
And the dark frogs chant in the safe morass,
And the sweetest stars are made to pass
   O'er the face of the darkest night.

6

But *we* who are dark, we are dark!
   Ah God, we have no stars!
About our souls in care and cark
   Our blackness shuts like prison-bars:
The poor souls crouch so far behind   40
That never a comfort can they find
   By reaching through the prison-bars.

7

Indeed we live beneath the sky,
    That great smooth Hand of God stretched out
On all His children fatherly,
    To save them from the dread and doubt
Which would be if, from this low place,
All opened straight up to His face
    Into the grand eternity.

8

And still God's sunshine and His frost,   50
    They make us hot, they make us cold,
As if we were not black and lost;
    And the beasts and birds, in wood and fold,
Do fear and take us for very men:
Could the whip-poor-will or the cat of the glen
    Look into my eyes and be bold?

9

I am black, I am black!
    But, once, I laughed in girlish glee,
For one of my colour stood in the track
    Where the drivers drove, and looked at me,   60
And tender and full was the look he gave –
Could a slave look so at another slave –
    I look at the sky and the sea.

10

And from that hour our spirits grew
    As free as if unsold, unbought:
Oh, strong enough, since we were two,
    To conquer the world, we thought.
The drivers drove us day by day;
We did not mind, we went one way,
    And no better a freedom sought.   70

11

In the sunny ground between the canes,
    He said 'I love you' as he passed;
When the shingle-roof rang sharp with the rains,

I heard how he vowed it fast:
While others shook he smiled in the hut,
As he carved me a bowl of the cocoa-nut
    Through the roar of the hurricanes.

12

I sang his name instead of a song,
    Over and over I sang his name,
Upward and downward I drew it along   80
    My various notes, – the same, the same!
I sang it low, that the slave-girls near
Might never guess, from aught they could hear,
    It was only a name – a name.

13

I look on the sky and the sea.
    We were two to love, and two to pray:
Yes, two, O God, who cried to Thee,
    Though nothing didst Thou say!
Coldly Thou sat'st behind the sun:
And now I cry who am but one,   90
    Thou wilt not speak to-day.

14

We were black, we were black,
    We had no claim to love and bliss,
What marvel if each went to wrack?
    They wrung my cold hands out of his,
They dragged him – where? I crawled to touch
His blood's mark in the dust . . . not much,
    Ye pilgrim-souls, though plain *as this*!

15

Wrong, followed by a deeper wrong!
    Mere grief's too good for such as I: 100
So the white men brought the shame ere long
    To strangle the sob of my agony.
They would not leave me for my dull
Wet eyes! – it was too merciful
    To let me weep pure tears and die.

16

I am black, I am black!
　I wore a child upon my breast,
An amulet that hung too slack,
　And, in my unrest, could not rest:
Thus we went moaning, child and mother,   110
One to another, one to another,
　Until all ended for the best.

17

For hark! I will tell you low, low,
　I am black, you see, –
And the babe who lay on my bosom so,
　Was far too white, too white for me;
As white as the ladies who scorned to pray
Beside me at church but yesterday,
　Though my tears had washed a place for my knee.

18

My own, own child! I could not bear   120
　To look in his face, it was so white;
I covered him up with a kerchief there,
　I covered his face in close and tight:
And he moaned and struggled, as well might be,
For the white child wanted his liberty –
　Ha, ha! he wanted the master-right.

19

He moaned and beat with his head and feet,
His little feet that never grew;
He struck them out, as it was meet,
　Against my heart to break it through: 130
I might have sung and made him mild,
But I dared not sing to the white-faced child
　The only song I knew.

20

I pulled the kerchief very close:
　He could not see the sun, I swear,
More, then, alive, than now he does

From between the roots of the mango . . . where?
I know where. Close! A child and mother
Do wrong to look at one another
　　When one is black and one is fair.   140

21

Why, in that single glance I had
　　Of my child's face, . . . I tell you all,
I saw a look that made me mad!
　　The *master's* look, that used to fall
On my soul like his lash . . . or worse!
And so, to save it from my curse,
　　I twisted it round in my shawl.

22

And he moaned and trembled from foot to head,
　　He shivered from head to foot;
Till after a time, he lay instead   150
　　Too suddenly still and mute.
I felt, beside, a stiffening cold:
I dared to lift up just a fold,
　　As in lifting a leaf of the mango-fruit.

23

But *my* fruit . . . ha, ha! – there, had been
　　(I laugh to think on't at this hour!)
Your fine white angels (who have seen
　　Nearest the secret of God's power)
And plucked my fruit to make them wine,
And sucked the soul of that child of mine   160
　　As the humming-bird sucks the soul of the flower.

24

Ha, ha, the trick of the angels white!
　　They freed the white child's spirit so.
I said not a word, but day and night
　　I carried the body to and fro,
And it lay on my heart like a stone, as chill.
– The sun may shine out as much as he will:
　　I am cold, though it happened a month ago.

25

From the white man's house, and the black man's hut,
   I carried the little body on;   170
The forest's arms did round us shut,
   And silence through the trees did run:
They asked no question as I went,
They stood too high for astonishment,
   They could see God sit on His throne.

26

My little body, kerchiefed fast,
   I bore it on through the forest, on;
And when I felt it was tired at last,
   I scooped a hole beneath the moon:
Through the forest-tops the angels far,   180
With a white sharp finger from every star,
   Did point and mock at what was done.

27

Yet when it was all done aright, –
   Earth, 'twixt me and my baby, strewed, –
All, changed to black earth – nothing white, –
   A dark child in the dark! – ensued
Some comfort, and my heart grew young;
I sate down smiling there and sung
   The song I learnt in my maidenhood.

28

And thus we two were reconciled,   190
   The white child and black mother, thus;
For as I sang it soft and wild,
   The same song, more melodious,
Rose from the grave where I sate:
It was the dead child singing that,
   To join the souls of both of us.

29

I look on the sea and the sky.
   Where the pilgrim's ships first anchored lay
The free sun rideth gloriously,

But the pilgrim-ghosts have slid away   200
Through the earliest streaks of the morn:
My face is black, but it glares with a scorn
   Which they dare not meet by day.

30

Ha! – in their stead, their hunter sons!
   Ha, ha! they are on me – they hunt in a ring!
Keep off! I brave you all at once,
   I throw off your eyes like snakes that sting!
You have killed the black eagle at nest, I think:
Did you ever stand still in your triumph, and shrink
   From the stroke of her wounded wing?   210

31

(Man, drop that stone you dared to lift! –)
   I wish you who stand there five abreast,
Each, for his own wife's joy and gift,
   A little corpse as safely at rest
As mine in the mangoes! Yes, but *she*
May keep live babies on her knee,
   And sing the song she likes the best.

32

I am not mad: I am black.
   I see you staring in my face –
I know you staring, shrinking back,   220
   Ye are born of the Washington-race,
And this land is the free America,
And this mark on my wrist – (I prove what I say)
   Ropes tied me up here to the flogging-place.

33

You think I shrieked then? Not a sound!
   I hung, as a gourd hangs in the sun;
I only cursed them all around
   As softly as I might have done
My very own child: from these sands
Up to the mountains, lift your hands,   230
   O slaves, and end what I begun!

34

Whips, curses; these must answer those!
   For in this Union you have set
Two kinds of men in adverse rows,
   Each loathing each; and all forget
The seven wounds in Christ's body fair,
While He sees gaping everywhere
   Our countless wounds that pay no debt.

35

Our wounds are different. Your white men
   Are, after all, not gods indeed,   240
Nor able to make Christs again
   Do good with bleeding. *We* who bleed
(Stand off!) we help not in our loss!
We are too heavy for our cross,
   And fall and crush you and your seed.

36

I fall, I swoon! I look at the sky.
   The clouds are breaking on my brain;
I am floated along, as if I should die
   Of liberty's exquisite pain.
In the name of the white child waiting for me   250
In the death-dark where we may kiss and agree,
White men, I leave you all curse-free
   In my broken heart's disdain!

Sonnets from the Portuguese

1

I thought once how Theocritus had sung
Of the sweet years, the dear and wished-for years,
Who each one in a gracious hand appears
To bear a gift for mortals, old or young:
And, as I mused it in his antique tongue,
I saw, in gradual vision through my tears,

The sweet, sad years, the melancholy years,
Those of my own life, who by turns had flung
A shadow across me. Straightway I was 'ware,
So weeping, how a mystic Shape did move   10
Behind me, and drew me backward by the hair;
And a voice said in mastery, while I strove, –
'Guess now who holds thee?' – 'Death,' I said. But, there,
The silver answer rang, – 'Not Death, but Love.'

                              2

But only three in all God's universe
Have heard this word thou hast said, – Himself, beside
Thee speaking, and me listening! and replied
One of us . . . *that* was God, . . . and laid the curse
So darkly on my eyelids, as to amerce
My sight from seeing thee, – that if I had died,
The death-weights, placed there, would have signified
Less absolute exclusion. 'Nay' is worse
From God than from all others, O my friend!
Men could not part us with their worldly jars,   10
Nor the seas change us, nor the tempests bend;
Our hands would touch for all the mountain-bars. –
And, heaven being rolled between us at the end,
We should but vow the faster for the stars.

                              3

Unlike are we, unlike, O princely Heart!
Unlike our uses and our destinies.
Our ministering two angels look surprise
On one another, as they strike athwart
Their wings in passing. Thou, bethink thee, art
A guest for queens to social pageantries,
With gages from a hundred brighter eyes
Than tears even can make mine, to play thy part
Of chief musician. What hast *thou* to do
With looking from the lattice-lights at me,   10
A poor, tired, wandering singer, . . . singing through
The dark, and leaning up a cypress tree?
The chrism is on thine head, – on mine, the dew, –
And Death must dig the level where these agree.

6

Go from me. Yet I feel that I shall stand
Henceforward in thy shadow. Nevermore
Alone upon the threshold of my door
Of individual life, I shall command
The uses of my soul, nor lift my hand
Serenely in the sunshine as before,
Without the sense of that which I forbore –
Thy touch upon the palm. The widest land
Doom takes to part us, leaves thy heart in mine
With pulses that beat double. What I do   10
And what I dream include thee, as the wine
Must taste of its own grapes. And when I sue
God for myself, He hears that name of thine,
And sees within my eyes the tears of two.

9

Can it be right to give what I can give?
To let thee sit beneath the fall of tears
As salt as mine, and hear the sighing years
Re-sighing on my lips renunciative
Through those infrequent smiles which fail to live
For all thy adjurations? O my fears,
That this can scarce be right! We are not peers,
So to be lovers; and I own, and grieve,
That givers of such gifts as mine are, must
Be counted with the ungenerous. Out, alas!   10
I will not soil thy purple with my dust,
Nor breathe my poison on thy Venice-glass,
Nor give thee any love – which were unjust.
Beloved, I only love thee! let it pass.

14

If thou must love me, let it be for nought
Except for love's sake only. Do not say
'I love her for her smile . . . her look . . . her way
Of speaking gently, . . . for a trick of thought
That falls in well with mine, and certes brought
A sense of pleasant ease on such a day' –
For these things in themselves, Belovèd, may

Be changed, or change for thee, – and love, so wrought
May be unwrought so. Neither love me for
Thine own dear pity's wiping my cheeks dry, –   10
A creature might forget to weep, who bore
Thy comfort long, and lose thy love thereby!
But love me for love's sake, that evermore
Thou may'st love on, through love's eternity.

17

My poet, thou canst touch on all the notes
God set between His After and Before,
And strike up and strike off the general roar
Of the rushing worlds a melody that floats
In a serene air purely. Antidotes
Of medicated music, answering for
Mankind's forlornest uses, thou canst pour
From thence into their ears. God's will devotes
Thine to such ends, and mine to wait on thine.
How, Dearest, wilt thou have me for most use?   10
A hope, to sing by gladly? . . . or a fine
Sad memory, with thy songs to interfuse?
A shade, in which to sing . . . of palm or pine?
A grave, on which to rest from singing? . . . Choose.

20

Belovèd, my Belovèd, when I think
That thou wast in the world a year ago,
What time I sat alone here in the snow
And saw no footprint, heard the silence sink
No moment at thy voice, . . . but, link by link,
Went counting all my chains as if that so
They never could fall off at any blow
Struck by thy possible hand . . . why, thus I drink
Of life's great cup of wonder! Wonderful,
Never to feel thee thrill the day or night   10
With personal act or speech, – nor even cull
Some prescience of thee with the blossoms white
Thou sawest growing! Atheists are as dull,
Who cannot guess God's presence out of sight.

21

Say over again, and yet once over again,
That thou dost love me. Though the word repeated
Should seem 'a cuckoo-song,' as thou dost treat it.
Remember, never to the hill or plain,
Valley and wood, without her cuckoo-strain
Comes the fresh Spring in all her green completed.
Belovèd, I, amid the darkness greeted
By a doubtful spirit-voice, in that doubt's pain
Cry, . . . 'Speak once more . . . thou lovest!' Who can fear
Too many stars, though each in heaven shall roll, –   10
Too many flowers, though each shall crown the year?
Say thou dost love me, love me, love me – toll
The silver iterance! – only minding, Dear,
To love me also in silence with thy soul.

22

When our two souls stand up erect and strong,
Face to face, silent, drawing nigh and nigher,
Until the lengthening wings break into fire
At either curvèd point, – what bitter wrong
Can the earth do to us, that we should not long
Be here contented? Think. In mounting higher,
The angels would press on us and aspire
To drop some golden orb of perfect song
Into our deep, dear silence. Let us stay
Rather on earth, Belovèd, – where the unfit   10
Contrarious moods of men recoil away
And isolate pure spirits, and permit
A place to stand and love in for a day,
With darkness and the death-hour rounding it.

23

Is it indeed so? If I lay here dead,
Wouldst thou miss any life in losing mine?
And would the sun for thee more coldly shine
Because of grave-damps falling round my head?
I marvelled, my Belovèd, when I read
Thy thought so in the letter. I am thine –
But . . . *so* much to thee? Can I pour thy wine

While my hands tremble? Then my soul, instead
Of dreams of death, resumes life's lower range.
Then, love me, Love! look on me . . . breathe on me!   10
As brighter ladies do not count it strange,
For love, to give up acres and degree,
I yield the grave for thy sake, and exchange
My near sweet view of heaven, for earth with thee!

24

Let the world's sharpness like a clasping knife
Shut in upon itself and do no harm
In this close hand of Love, now soft and warm,
And let us hear no sound of human strife
After the click of the shutting. Life to life –
I lean upon thee, Dear, without alarm,
And feel as safe as guarded by a charm
Against the stab of worldlings, who if rife
Are weak to injure. Very whitely still
The lilies of our lives may reassure   10
Their blossoms from their roots, accessible
Alone to heavenly dews that drop not fewer:
Growing straight, out of man's reach, on the hill.
God only, who made us rich, can make us poor.

26

I lived with visions for my company
Instead of men and women, years ago,
And found them gentle mates, nor thought to know
A sweeter music than they played to me.
But soon their trailing purple was not free
Of this world's dust, – their lutes did silent grow,
And I myself grew faint and blind below
Their vanishing eyes. Then THOU didst come . . . to be,
Belovèd, what they seemed. Their shining fronts,
Their songs, their splendours, (better, yet the same,   10
As river-water hallowed into fonts)
Met in thee, and from out thee overcame
My soul with satisfaction of all wants –
Because God's gift put man's best dreams to shame.

28

My letters! all dead paper, . . . mute and white!
And yet they seem alive and quivering
Against my tremulous hands which loose the string
And let them drop down on my knee to-night.
This said, . . . he wished to have me in his sight
Once, as a friend: this fixed a day in spring
To come and touch my hand . . . a simple thing,
Yet I wept for it! – this, . . . the paper's light . . .
Said, *Dear I love thee*; and I sank and quailed
As if God's future thundered on my past.   10
This said, *I am thine* – and so its ink has paled
With lying at my heart that beat too fast.
And this . . . O Love, thy words have ill availed
If, what this said, I dared repeat at last!

38

First time he kissed me, he but only kissed
The fingers of the hand wherewith I write;
And ever since, it grew more clean and white, . . .
Slow to world-greetings, quick with its 'Oh, list,'
When the angels speak. A ring of amethyst
I could not wear here, plainer to my sight,
Than that first kiss. The second passed in height
The first, and sought the forehead, and half missed,
Half falling on the hair. O beyond meed!
That was the chrism of love, which love's own crown   10
With sanctifying sweetness, did precede.
The third upon my lips was folded down
In perfect, purple state; since when, indeed,
I have been proud and said, 'My love, my own.'

42

'*My future will not copy fair my past*' –
I wrote that once; and thinking at my side
My ministering life-angel justified
The word by his appealing look upcast
To the white throne of God, I turned at last,
And there, instead, saw thee, not unallied
To angels in thy soul! Then I, long tried

By natural ills, received the comfort fast,
While budding, at thy sight, my pilgrim's staff
Gave out green leaves with morning dews impearled.   10
I seek no copy now of life's first half:
Leave here the pages with long musing curled,
And write me new my future's epigraph,
New angel mine, unhoped for in the world!

                              43

How do I love thee? Let me count the ways.
I love thee to the depth and breadth and height
My soul can reach, when feeling out of sight
For the ends of Being and ideal Grace.
I love thee to the level of everyday's
Most quiet need, by sun and candlelight.
I love thee freely, as men strive for Right;
I love thee purely, as they turn from Praise.
I love thee with the passion put to use
In my old griefs, and with my childhood's faith.   10
I love thee with a love I seemed to lose
With my lost saints, – I love thee with the breath,
Smiles, tears, of all my life! – and, if God choose,
I shall but love thee better after death.

                              44

Belovèd, thou hast brought me many flowers
Plucked in the garden, all the summer through
And winter, and it seemed as if they grew
In this close room, nor missed the sun and showers.
So, in the like name of that love of ours,
Take back these thoughts which here unfolded too,
And which on warm and cold days I withdrew
From my heart's ground. Indeed, those beds and bowers
Be overgrown with bitter weeds and rue,
And wait thy weeding; yet here's eglantine,   10
Here's ivy! – take them, as I used to do
Thy flowers, and keep them where they shall not pine.
Instruct thine eyes to keep their colours true,
And tell thy soul, their roots are left in mine.

Casa Guidi Windows

PART ONE

I heard last night a little child go singing
   'Neath Casa Guidi windows, by the church,
O bella libertà, O bella! stringing
   The same words still on notes he went in search
So high for, you concluded the upspringing
   Of such a nimble bird to sky from perch
Must leave the whole bush in a tremble green,
   And that the heart of Italy must beat,
While such a voice had leave to rise serene
   'Twixt church and palace of a Florence street!   10
A little child, too, who not long had been
   By mother's finger steadied on his feet,
And still *O bella libertà* he sang.

Then I thought, musing, of the innumerous
   Sweet songs which still for Italy outrang
From older singers' lips, who sang not thus
   Exultingly and purely, yet, with pang
Fast sheathed in music, touched the heart of us
   So finely, that the pity scarcely pained.
I thought how Filicaja led on others,   20
   Bewailers for their Italy enchained,
And how they called her childless among mothers,
   Widow of empires, aye, and scarce refrained
Cursing her beauty to her face, as brothers
   Might a shamed sister's, – 'Had she been less fair
She were less wretched,' – how, evoking so
   From congregated wrong and heaped despair
Of men and women writhing under blow,
   Harrowed and hideous in a filthy lair,
Some personating Image, wherein woe   30
   Was wrapt in beauty from offending much,
They called it Cybele, or Niobe,
   Or laid it corpse-like on a bier for such,
Where all the world might drop for Italy

Those cadenced tears which burn not where they touch, –
'Juliet of nations, canst thou die as we?
    And was the violet crown that crowned thy head
So over-large, though new buds made it rough,
    It slipped down and across thine eyelids dead,
O sweet, fair Juliet?' Of such songs enough,   40
    Too many of such complaints! behold, instead,
Void at Verona, Juliet's marble trough.
    As void as that is, are all images
Men set between themselves and actual wrong,
    To catch the weight of pity, meet the stress
Of conscience, – since 'tis easier to gaze long
    On mournful masks, and sad effigies,
Than on real, live, weak creatures crushed by strong.

    For me who stand in Italy to-day,
Where worthier poets stood and sang before,   50
    I kiss their footsteps, yet their words gainsay.
I can but muse in hope upon this shore
    Of golden Arno as it shoots away
Through Florence' heart beneath her bridges four!
    Bent bridges, seeming to strain off like bows,
And tremble while the arrowy undertide
    Shoots on and cleaves the marble as it goes,
And strikes up palace-walls on either side,
    And froths the cornice out in glittering rows,
With doors and windows quaintly multiplied,   60
    And terrace-sweeps, and gazers upon all,
By whom if flower or kerchief were thrown out
    From any lattice there, the same would fall
Into the river underneath no doubt,
    It runs so close and fast 'twixt wall and wall.
How beautiful! the mountains from without
    In silence listen for the word said next.
What word will men say, – here where Giotto planted
    His campanile, like an unperplexed
Fine question Heaven-ward, touching the things granted   70
    A noble people who, being greatly vexed
In act, in aspiration keep undaunted?
    What word will God say? Michel's Night and Day

And Dawn and Twilight wait in marble scorn,
   Like dogs upon a dunghill, couched on clay
From whence the Medicean stamp's outworn,
   The final putting off of all such sway
By all such hands, and freeing of the unborn
   In Florence and the great world outside Florence.
Three hundred years his patient statues wait   80
   In that small chapel of the dim St Lawrence.
Day's eyes are breaking bold and passionate
   Over his shoulder, and will flash abhorrence
On darkness and with level looks meet fate,
   When once loose from that marble film of theirs;
The Night has wild dreams in her sleep, the Dawn
   Is haggard as the sleepless, Twilight wears
A sort of horror; as the veil withdrawn
   'Twixt the artist's soul and works had left them heirs
Of speechless thoughts which would not quail nor fawn,   90
   Of angers and contempts, of hope and love;
For not without a meaning did he place
   The princely Urbino on the seat above
With everlasting shadow on his face,
   While the slow dawns and twilights disapprove
The ashes of his long-extinguished race,
   Which never more shall clog the feet of men.
I do believe, divinest Angelo,
   That winter-hour, in Via Larga, when
They bade thee build a statue up in snow,   100
   And straight that marvel of thine art again
Dissolved beneath the sun's Italian glow,
   Thine eyes, dilated with the plastic passion,
Thawing too, in drops of wounded manhood, since,
   To mock alike thine art and indignation,
Laughed at the palace-window the new prince, –
   ('Aha! this genius needs for exaltation,
When all's said, and howe'er the proud may wince,
   A little marble from our princely mines!')
I do believe that hour thou laughedst too,   110
   For the whole sad world and for thy Florentines,
After those few tears – which were only few!
   That as, beneath the sun, the grand white lines

Of thy snow-statue trembled and withdrew, –
  The head, erect as Jove's, being palsied first,
The eyelids flattened, the full brow turned blank, –
  The right hand, raised but now as if it cursed,
Dropt, a mere snowball, (till the people sank
  Their voices, though a louder laughter burst
From the royal window) thou couldst proudly thank   120
  God and the prince for promise and presage,
And laugh the laugh back, I think verily,
  Thine eyes being purged by tears of righteous rage
To read a wrong into a prophecy,
  And measure a true great man's heritage
Against a mere great duke's posterity.
  I think thy soul said then, 'I do not need
A princedom and its quarries, after all;
  For if I write, paint, carve a word, indeed,
On book or board or dust, on floor or wall,   130
  The same is kept of God, who taketh heed
That not a letter of the meaning fall
  Or ere it touch and teach His world's deep heart,
Outlasting, therefore, all your lordships, sir!
  So keep your stone, beseech you, for your part,
To cover up your grave-place and refer
  The proper titles; I live by my art.
The thought I threw into this snow shall stir
  This gazing people when their gaze is done;
And the tradition of your act and mine   140
  When all the snow is melted in the sun,
Shall gather up, for unborn men, a sign
  Of what is the true princedom, – aye, and none
Shall laugh that day, except the drunk with wine.'

  Amen, great Angelo! the day's at hand.
If many laugh not on it, shall we weep?
  Much more we must not, let us understand.
Through rhymers sonneteering in their sleep,
  And archaists mumbling dry bones up the land,
And sketchers lauding ruined towns a-heap, –   150
  Through all that drowsy hum of voices smooth,
The hopeful bird mounts carolling from brake,

The hopeful child, with leaps to catch his growth,
Sings open-eyed for liberty's sweet sake!
  And I, a singer also, from my youth,
Prefer to sing with these who are awake,
    With birds, with babes, with men who will not fear
The baptism of the holy morning dew,
    (And many of such wakers now are here,
Complete in their anointed manhood, who   160
    Will greatly dare and greatlier persevere,)
Than join those old thin voices with my new,
    And sigh for Italy with some safe sigh
Cooped up in music 'twixt an oh and ah, –
    Nay, hand in hand with that young child, will I
Go singing rather, '*Bella libertà*,'
    Than, with those poets, croon the dead or cry
'*Se tu men bella fossi, Italia!*'

  'Less wretched if less fair.' Perhaps a truth
Is so far plain in this – that Italy,   170
    Long trammelled with the purple of her youth
Against her age's ripe activity,
    Sits still upon her tombs, without death's ruth,
But also without life's brave energy.
    'Now tell us what is Italy?' men ask:
And others answer, 'Virgil, Cicero,
    Catullus, Cæsar.' What beside? to task
The memory closer – 'Why, Boccaccio,
    Dante, Petrarca,' – and if still the flask
Appears to yield its wine by drops too slow, –   180
    'Angelo, Raffael, Pergolese,' – all
Whose strong hearts beat through stone, or charged again
    The paints with fire of souls electrical,
Or broke up heaven for music. What more then?
    Why, then, no more. The chaplet's last beads fall
In naming the last saintship within ken,
    And, after that, none prayeth in the land.
Alas, this Italy has too long swept
    Heroic ashes up for hour-glass sand;
Of her own past, impassioned nympholept!   190
    Consenting to be nailed here by the hand

To the very bay-tree under which she stepped
  A queen of old, and plucked a leafy branch.
And, licensing the world too long indeed
  To use her broad phylacteries to staunch
And stop her bloody lips, she takes no heed
  How one clear word would draw an avalanche
Of living sons around her, to succeed
  The vanished generations. Can she count
These oil-eaters, with large, live, mobile mouths   200
  Agape for maccaroni, in the amount
Of consecrated heroes of her south's
  Bright rosary? The pitcher at the fount,
The gift of gods, being broken, she much loathes
  To let the ground-leaves of the place confer
A natural bowl. So henceforth she would seem
  No nation, but the poet's pensioner,
With alms from every land of song and dream,
  While aye her pipers sadly pipe of her,
Until their proper breaths, in that extreme   210
  Of sighing, split the reed on which they played!
Of which, no more. But never say 'no more'
  To Italy's life! Her memories undismayed
Still 'evermore,' – her graves implore
  Her future to be strong and not afraid;
Her very statues send their looks before.

We do not serve the dead – the past is past!
God lives, and lifts his glorious mornings up
  Before the eyes of men, awake at last,
Who put away the meats they used to sup,   220
  And down upon the dust of earth outcast
The dregs remaining of the ancient cup,
  Then turn to wakeful prayer and worthy act.
The dead, upon their awful 'vantage ground,
  The sun not in their faces, – shall abstract
No more our strength: we will not be discrowned
  As guardians of their crowns; nor deign transact
A barter of the present, for a sound
  Of good, so counted in the foregone days.
O Dead, ye shall no longer cling to us   230

With rigid hands of desiccating praise,
And drag us backward by the garment thus,
    To stand and laud you in long-drawn virelays!
We will not henceforth be oblivious
    Of our own lives, because ye lived before,
Nor of our acts, because ye acted well.
    We thank you that ye first unlatched the door,
But will not make it inaccessible
    By thankings on the threshold any more.
We hurry onward to extinguish hell   240
    With our fresh souls, our younger hope, and God's
Maturity of purpose. Soon shall we
    Die also! and, that then our periods
Of life may round themselves to memory,
    As smoothly as on our graves the burial-sods,
We now must look to it to excel as ye,
    And bear our age as far, unlimited
By the last mind-mark! so, to be invoked
    By future generations, as their Dead.

'Tis true that when the dust of death has choked   250
    A great man's voice, the common words he said
Turn oracles, – the common thoughts he yoked
    Like horses, draw like griffins! – this is true
And acceptable. I, too, should desire,
    When men make record, with the flowers they strew,
'Savonarola's soul went out in fire
    Upon our Grand-duke's piazza, and burned through
A moment first, or ere he did expire,
    The veil betwixt the right and wrong, and showed
How near God sate and judged the judges there, –'   260
    Upon the self-same pavement overstrewed,
To cast my violets with as reverent care,
    And prove that all the winters which have snowed
Cannot snow out the scent from stones and air,
    Of a sincere man's virtues. This was he,
Savonarola, who, while Peter sank
    With his whole boat-load, called courageously
'Wake Christ, wake Christ!' – Who, having tried the tank
    Of old church-waters used for baptistry

Ere Luther came to spill them, swore they stank!   270
    Who also by a princely deathbed cried,
'Loose Florence, or God will not loose thy soul!'
    Then fell back the Magnificent and died
Beneath the star-look, shooting from the cowl,
    Which turned to wormwood bitterness the wide
Deep sea of his ambitions. It were foul
    To grudge Savonarola and the rest
Their violets! rather pay them quick and fresh!
    The emphasis of death makes manifest
The eloquence of action in our flesh;   280
    And men who, living, were but dimly guessed,
When once free from their life's entangled mesh,
    Show their full length in graves, or oft indeed
Exaggerate their stature, in the flat,
    To noble admirations which exceed
Most nobly, yet will calculate in that
    But accurately. We, who are the seed
Of buried creatures, if we turned and spat
    Upon our antecedents, we were vile.
Bring violets rather! If these had not walked   290
    Their furlong, could we hope to walk our mile?
Therefore bring violets. Yet if we, self-baulked,
    Stand still, a-strewing violets all the while,
These moved in vain, of whom we have vainly talked.
    So rise up henceforth with a cheerful smile,
And having strewn the violets, reap the corn,
    And having reaped and garnered, bring the plough
And draw new furrows 'neath the healthy morn,
    And plant the great Hereafter in this Now.

Of old 'twas so. How step by step was worn,   300
    As each man gained on each, securely! – how
Each by his own strength sought his own ideal, –
    The ultimate Perfection leaning bright
From out the sun and stars, to bless the leal
    And earnest search of all for Fair and Right,
Through doubtful forms, by earth accounted real!
    Because old Jubal blew into delight
The souls of men, with clear-piped melodies,

If youthful Asaph were content at most
To draw from Jubal's grave, with listening eyes,   310
   Traditionary music's floating ghost
Into the grass-grown silence, were it wise?
   And was't not wiser, Jubal's breath being lost,
That Miriam clashed her cymbals to surprise
   The sun between her white arms flung apart,
With new, glad, golden sounds? that David's strings
   O'erflowed his hand with music from his heart?
So harmony grows full from many springs,
   And happy accident turns holy art.

You enter, in your Florence wanderings,   320
   The church of St Maria Novella. Pass
The left stair, where at plague-time Macchiavel
   Saw One with set fair face as in a glass,
Dressed out against the fear of death and hell,
   Rustling her silks in pauses of the mass,
To keep the thought off how her husband fell,
   When she left home, stark dead across her feet, –
The stair leads up to what the Orgagnas save
   Of Dante's dæmons; you, in passing it,
Ascend the right stair from the farther nave,   330
   To muse in a small chapel scarcely lit
By Cimabue's Virgin. Bright and brave,
   That picture was accounted, mark, of old.
A king stood bare before its sovran grave,
   A reverent people shouted to behold
The picture, not the king, and even the place
   Containing such a miracle, grew bold,
Named the Glad Borgo from that beauteous face, –
   Which thrilled the artist, after work, to think
His own ideal Mary-smile should stand   340
   So very near him, – he, within the brink
Of all that glory, let in by his hand
   With too divine a rashness! Yet none shrink
Who come to gaze here now – albeit 'twas planned
   Sublimely in the thought's simplicity.
The Lady, throned in empyreal state,
   Minds only the young babe upon her knee,

While sidelong angels bear the royal weight,
   Prostrated meekly, smiling tenderly
Oblivion of their wings; the Child thereat   350
   Stretching its hand like God. If any should,
Because of some stiff draperies and loose joints,
   Gaze scorn down from the heights of Raffaelhood,
On Cimabue's picture, – Heaven anoints
   The head of no such critic, and his blood
The poet's curse strikes full on and appoints
   To ague and cold spasms for evermore.
A noble picture! worthy of the shout
   Wherewith along the streets the people bore
Its cherub faces, which the sun threw out   360
   Until they stooped and entered the church door! –
Yet rightly was young Giotto talked about,
   Whom Cimabue found among the sheep,
And knew, as gods know gods, and carried home
   To paint the things he had painted, with a deep
And fuller insight, and so overcome
   His chapel-lady with a heavenlier sweep
Of light. For thus we mount into the sum
   Of great things known or acted. I hold, too,
That Cimabue smiled upon the lad,   370
   At the first stroke which passed what he could do, –
Or else this Virgin's smile had never had
   Such sweetness in't. All great men who foreknew
Their heirs in art, for art's sake have been glad,
   And bent their old white heads as if uncrowned,
Fanatics of their pure ideals still
   Far more than of their triumphs, which were found
With some less vehement struggle of the will.
   If old Margheritone trembled, swooned,
And died despairing at the open sill   380
   Of other men's achievements, (who achieved,
By loving art beyond the master!) he
   Was old Margheritone, and conceived
Never, at first youth and most ecstasy,
   A Virgin like that dream of one, which heaved
The death-sigh from his heart. If wistfully
   Margheritone sickened at the smell

Of Cimabue's laurel, let him go! –
　　For Cimabue stood up very well
In spite of Giotto's – and Angelico,   390
　　The artist-saint, kept smiling in his cell
The smile with which he welcomed the sweet slow
　　Inbreak of angels, (whitening through the dim
That he might paint them!) while the sudden sense
　　Of Raffael's future was revealed to him
By force of his own fair works' competence.
　　The same blue waters where the dolphins swim
Suggest the tritons. Through the blue Immense,
　　Strike out, all swimmers! cling not in the way
Of one another, so to sink; but learn   400
　　The strong man's impulse, catch the fresh'ning spray
He throws up in his motions, and discern
　　By his clear, westering eye, the time of day.
Thou, God, hast set us worthy gifts to earn,
　　Besides thy heaven and Thee! and when I say
There's room here for the weakest man alive
　　To live and die, – there's room too, I repeat,
For all the strongest to live well, and strive
　　Their own way, by their individual heat, –
Like some new bee-swarm leaving the old hive,   410
　　Despite the wax which tempts so violet-sweet.
Then let the living live, the dead retain
　　Their grave-cold flowers! – though honour's best supplied,
By bringing actions, to prove theirs not vain.

Cold graves, we say? It shall be testified
That living men who burn in heart and brain,
　　Without the dead were colder. If we tried
To sink the past beneath our feet, be sure
　　The future would not stand. Precipitate
This old roof from the shrine – and, insecure,   420
　　The nesting swallows fly off, mate from mate.
How scant the gardens, if the graves were fewer!
　　The tall green poplars grew no longer straight,
Whose tops not looked to Troy. Would any fight
　　For Athens, and not swear by Marathon?
Who dared build temples, without tombs in sight?

Or live, without some dead man's benison?
Or seek truth, hope for good, and strive for right,
    If, looking up, he saw not in the sun
Some angel of the martyrs all day long   430
    Standing and waiting? Your last rhythm will need
Your earliest key-note. Could I sing this song,
    If my dead masters had not taken heed
To help the heavens and earth to make me strong,
    As the wind ever will find out some reed,
And touch it to such issues as belong
    To such a frail thing? None may grudge the dead,
Libations from full cups. Unless we choose
    To look back to the hills behind us spread,
The plains before us, sadden and confuse;   440
    If orphaned, we are disinherited.

I would but turn these lachrymals to use,
    And pour fresh oil in from the olive grove,
To furnish them as new lamps. Shall I say
    What made my heart beat with exulting love,
A few weeks back? –
                              . . . The day was such a day
    As Florence owes the sun. The sky above,
Its weight upon the mountains seemed to lay,
    And palpitate in glory, like a dove
Who has flown too fast, full-hearted! – take away   450
    The image! for the heart of man beat higher
That day in Florence, flooding all her streets
    And piazzas with a tumult and desire.
The people, with accumulated heats,
    And faces turned one way, as if one fire
Both drew and flushed them, left their ancient beats,
    And went up toward the palace-Pitti wall,
To thank their Grand-duke, who, not quite of course,
    Had graciously permitted, at their call,
The citizens to use their civic force   460
    To guard their civic homes. So, one and all,
The Tuscan cities streamed up to the source
    Of this new good, at Florence, taking it
As good so far, presageful of more good, –

The first torch of Italian freedom, lit
To toss in the next tiger's face who should
   Approach too near them in a greedy fit, –
The first pulse of an even flow of blood,
   To prove the level of Italian veins
Toward rights perceived and granted. How we gazed   470
   From Casa Guidi windows, while, in trains
Of orderly procession – banners raised,
   And intermittent burst of martial strains
Which died upon the shout, as if amazed
   By gladness beyond music – they passed on!
The Magistracy, with insignia, passed, –
   And all the people shouted in the sun,
And all the thousand windows which had cast
   A ripple of silks, in blue and scarlet, down,
(As if the houses overflowed at last),   480
   Seemed growing larger with fair heads and eyes.
The Lawyers passed, – and still arose the shout,
   And hands broke from the windows to surprise
Those grave calm brows with bay-tree leaves thrown out.
   The Priesthood passed, – the friars with worldly-wise
Keen sidelong glances from their beards about
   The street to see who shouted! many a monk
Who takes a long rope in the waist, was there!
   Whereat the popular exultation drunk
With indrawn 'vivas' the whole sunny air,   490
   While, through the murmuring windows, rose and sunk
A cloud of kerchiefed hands, – 'The church makes fair
   Her welcome in the new Pope's name.' Ensued
The black sign of the 'Martyrs!' (name no name,
   But count the graves in silence.) Next, were viewed
The Artists; next, the Trades; and after came
   The People, – flag and sign, and rights as good, –
And very loud the shout was for that same
   Motto, 'Il popolo.' IL POPOLO, –
The word means dukedom, empire, majesty,   500
   And kings in such an hour might read it so.
And next, with banners, each in his degree,
   Deputed representatives a-row
Of every separate state of Tuscany.

Siena's she-wolf, bristling on the fold
Of the first flag, preceded Pisa's hare,
   And Massa's lion floated calm in gold,
Pienza's followed with his silver stare.
   Arezzo's steed pranced clear from bridle-hold, –
And well might shout our Florence, greeting there   510
   These, and more brethren. Last, the world had sent
The various children of her teeming flanks –
   Greeks, English, French – as if to a parliament
Of lovers of her Italy in ranks,
   Each bearing its land's symbol reverent.
At which the stones seemed breaking into thanks
   And rattling up the sky, such sounds in proof
Arose; the very house-walls seemed to bend;
   The very windows, up from door to roof,
Flashed out a rapture of bright heads, to mend   520
   With passionate looks, the gesture's whirling off
A hurricane of leaves. Three hours did end
   While all these passed; and ever in the crowd,
Rude men, unconscious of the tears that kept
   Their beards moist, shouted; some few laughed aloud,
And none asked any why they laughed and wept.
   Friends kissed each other's cheeks, and foes long vowed
More warmly did it, – two-months' babies leapt
   Right upward in their mother's arms, whose black,
Wide, glittering eyes looked elsewhere; lovers pressed   530
   Each before either, neither glancing back;
And peasant maidens, smoothly 'tired and tressed,
   Forgot to finger on their throats the slack
Great pearl-strings; while old blind men would not rest,
   But pattered with their staves and slid their shoes
Along the stones, and smiled as if they saw.
   O heaven, I think that day had noble use
Among God's days. So near stood Right and Law,
   Both mutually forborne! Law would not bruise,
Nor Right deny, and each in reverent awe   540
   Honoured the other. And if, ne'ertheless,
That good day's sun delivered to the vines
   No charta, and the liberal Duke's excess
Did scarce exceed a Guelf's or Ghibelline's

In any special actual righteousness
Of what that day he granted, still the signs
    Are good and full of promise, we must say,
When multitudes approach their kings with prayers
    And kings concede their people's right to pray,
Both in one sunshine. Griefs are not despairs,   550
    So uttered, nor can royal claims dismay
When men from humble homes and ducal chairs,
    Hate wrong together. It was well to view
Those banners ruffled in a ruler's face
    Inscribed, 'Live freedom, union, and all true
Brave patriots who are aided by God's grace!'
    Nor was it ill, when Leopoldo drew
His little children to the window-place
    He stood in at the Pitti, to suggest
They too should govern as the people willed.   560
    What a cry rose then! some, who saw the best,
Declared his eyes filled up and overfilled
    With good warm human tears which unrepressed
Ran down. I like his face; the forehead's build
    Has no capacious genius, yet perhaps
Sufficient comprehension, – mild and sad,
    And careful nobly, not with care that wraps
Self-loving hearts, to stifle and make mad,
    But careful with the care that shuns a lapse
Of faith and duty, studious not to add   570
    A burden in the gathering of a gain.
And so, God save the Duke, I say with those
    Who that day shouted it, and while dukes reign,
May all wear in the visible overflows
    Of spirit, such a look of careful pain!
For God must love it better than repose.

And all the people who went up to let
    Their hearts out to that Duke, as has been told –
Where guess ye that the living people met,
    Kept tryst, formed ranks, chose leaders, first unrolled   580
Their banners?
                    In the Loggia? where is set
    Cellini's godlike Perseus, bronze – or gold –

(How name the metal, when the statue flings
   Its soul so in your eyes?) with brow and sword
Superbly calm, as all opposing things,
   Slain with the Gorgon, were no more abhorred
Since ended?
             No, the people sought no wings
   From Perseus in the Loggia, nor implored
An inspiration in the place beside,
   From that dim bust of Brutus, jagged and grand,   590
Where Buonarroti passionately tried
   From out the close-clenched marble to demand
The head of Rome's sublimest homicide, –
   Then dropt the quivering mallet from his hand,
Despairing he could find no model-stuff
   Of Brutus, in all Florence, where he found
The gods and gladiators thick enough.
   Nor there! the people chose still holier ground!
The people, who are simple, blind, and rough,
   Know their own angels, after looking round.   600
Whom chose they then? where met they?

                        On the stone
   Called Dante's, – a plain flat stone, scarce discerned
From others in the pavement, – whereupon
   He used to bring his quiet chair out, turned
To Brunelleschi's church, and pour alone
   The lava of his spirit when it burned.
It is not cold to-day. O passionate
   Poor Dante, who, a banished Florentine,
Didst sit austere at banquets of the great,
   And muse upon this far-off stone of thine,   610
And think how oft some passer used to wait
   A moment, in the golden day's decline,
With 'Good night, dearest Dante!' – well, good night!
   I muse now, Dante, and think, verily,
Though chapelled in the byeway, out of sight,
   Ravenna's bones would thrill with ecstasy,
Could'st know thy favourite stone's elected right
   As tryst-place for thy Tuscans to foresee
Their earliest chartas from. Good night, good morn,

Henceforward, Dante! now my soul is sure 620
That thine is better comforted of scorn,
  And looks down earthward in completer cure,
Than when, in Santa Croce church forlorn
  Of any corpse, the architect and hewer
Did pile the empty marbles as thy tomb.
  For now thou art no longer exiled, now
Best honoured! – we salute thee who art come
  Back to the old stone with a softer brow
Than Giotto drew upon the wall, for some
  Good lovers of our age to track and plough 630
Their way to, through time's ordures stratified,
  And startle broad awake into the dull
Bargello chamber! now, thou'rt milder eyed, –
  Now Beatrix may leap up glad to cull
Thy first smile, even in heaven and at her side,
  Like that which, nine years old, looked beautiful
At May-game. What do I say? I only meant
  That tender Dante loved his Florence well,
While Florence, now, to love him is content;
  And, mark ye, that the piercingest sweet smell 640
Of love's dear incense by the living sent
  To find the dead, is not accessible
To lazy livers! no narcotic, – not
  Swung in a censer to a sleepy tune, –
But trod out in the morning air, by hot
  Quick spirits, who tread firm to ends foreshown,
And use the name of greatness unforgot,
  To meditate what greatness may be done.

For Dante sits in heaven, and ye stand here,
  And more remains for doing, all must feel, 650
Than trysting on his stone from year to year
  To shift processions, civic toe to heel,
The town's thanks to the Pitti. Are ye freer
  For what was felt that day? a chariot-wheel
May spin fast, yet the chariot never roll.
  But if that day suggested something good,
And bettered, with one purpose, soul by soul, –
  Better means freer. A land's brotherhood
Is most puissant: men, upon the whole,

Are what they can be, – nations, what they would.   660

Will, therefore, to be strong, thou Italy!
    Will to be noble! Austrian Metternich
Can fix no yoke unless the neck agree;
    And thine is like the lion's when the thick
Dews shudder from it, and no man would be
    The stroker of his mane, much less would prick
His nostril with a reed. When nations roar
    Like lions, who shall tame them, and defraud
Of the due pasture by the river-shore?
    Roar, therefore! shake your dew-laps dry abroad.   670
The amphitheatre with open door
    Leads back upon the benchers, who applaud
The last spear-thruster.
                            Yet the Heavens forbid
    That we should call on passion to confront
The brutal with the brutal, and, amid
    This ripening world, suggest a lion's-hunt
And lion's-vengeance for the wrongs men did
    And do now, though the spears are getting blunt.
We only call, because the sight and proof
    Of lion-strength hurts nothing; and to show   680
A lion-heart, and measure paw with hoof,
    Helps something, even, and will instruct a foe
As well as the onslaught, how to stand aloof!
    Or else the world gets past the mere brute blow
Or given or taken. Children use the fist
    Until they are of age to use the brain;
And so we needed Cæsars to assist
    Man's justice, and Napoleons to explain
God's counsel, when a point was nearly missed,
    Until our generations should attain   690
Christ's stature nearer. Not that we, alas,
    Attain already; but a single inch
Will raise to look down on the swordsman's pass,
    As knightly Roland on the coward's flinch:
And, after chloroform and ether-gas,
    We find out slowly what the bee and finch
Have ready found, through Nature's lamp in each,

How to our races we may justify
Our individual claims, and, as we reach
    Our own grapes, bend the top vines to supply   700
The children's uses, – how to fill a breach
    With olive branches, – how to quench a lie
With truth, and smite a foe upon the cheek
    With Christ's most conquering kiss. Why, these are things
Worth a great nation's finding, to prove weak
    The 'glorious arms' of military kings.
And so with wide embrace, my England, seek
    To stifle the bad heat and flickerings
Of this world's false and nearly expended fire!
    Draw palpitating arrows to the wood,   710
And twang abroad thy high hopes, and thy higher
    Resolves, from the most virtuous altitude!
Till nations shall unconsciously aspire
    By looking up to thee, and learn that good
And glory are not different. Announce law
    By freedom; exalt chivalry by peace;
Instruct how clear calm eyes can overawe,
    And how pure hands, stretched simply to release
A bond-slave, will not need a sword to draw
    To be held dreadful. O my England, crease   720
Thy purple with no alien agonies!
    No struggles toward encroachment, no vile war!
Disband thy captains, change thy victories,
    Be henceforth prosperous as the angels are,
Helping, not humbling.

                              Drums and battle cries
    Go out in music of the morning star –
And soon we shall have thinkers in the place
    Of fighters, each found able as a man
To strike electric influence through a race,
    Unstayed by city-wall and barbican.   730
The poet shall look grander in the face
    Than even of old, (when he of Greece began
To sing 'that Achillean wrath which slew
    So many heroes,') – seeing he shall treat
The deeds of souls heroic toward the true –

The oracles of life – previsions sweet
And awful, like divine swans gliding through
     White arms of Ledas, which will leave the heat
Of their escaping godship to endue
     The human medium with a heavenly flush.   740

Meanwhile, in this same Italy we want
     Not popular passion, to arise and crush,
But popular conscience, which may covenant
     For what it knows. Concede without a blush,
To grant the 'civic guard' is not to grant
     The civic spirit, living and awake.
Those lappets on your shoulders, citizens,
     Your eyes strain after sideways till they ache,
(While still, in admirations and amens,
     The crowd comes up on festa-days, to take   750
The great sight in) – are not intelligence,
     Not courage even – alas, if not the sign
Of something very noble, they are nought;
     For every day ye dress your sallow kine
With fringes down their cheeks, though unbesought
     They loll their heavy heads and drag the wine,
And bear the wooden yoke as they were taught
     The first day. What ye want is light – indeed
Not sunlight – (ye may well look up surprised
     To those unfathomable heavens that feed   760
Your purple hills!) – but God's light organised
     In some high soul, crowned capable to lead
The conscious people, conscious and advised, –
     For if we lift a people like mere clay,
It falls the same. We want thee, O unfound
     And sovran teacher! – if thy beard be grey
Or black, we bid thee rise up from the ground
     And speak the word God giveth thee to say,
Inspiring into all this people round,
     Instead of passion, thought, which pioneers   770
All generous passion, purifies from sin,
     And strikes the hour for. Rise up teacher! here's
A crowd to make a nation! – best begin
     By making each a man, till all be peers

Of earth's true patriots and pure martyrs in
   Knowing and daring. Best unbar the doors
Which Peter's heirs keep locked so overclose
   They only let the mice across the floors,
While every churchman dangles, as he goes,
   The great key at his girdle, and abhors   780
In Christ's name, meekly. Open wide the house,
   Concede the entrance with Christ's liberal mind,
And set the tables with His wine and bread.
   What! 'commune in both kinds?' In every kind –
Wine, wafer, love, hope, truth, unlimited,
   Nothing kept back. For when a man is blind
To starlight, will he see the rose is red?
   A bondsman shivering at a Jesuit's foot –
'Væ! meâ culpâ!' is not like to stand
   A freedman at a despot's, and dispute   790
His titles by the balance in his hand,
   Weighing them 'suo jure.' Tend the root
If careful of the branches, and expand
   The inner souls of men before you strive
For civic heroes.

                But the teacher, where?
   From all these crowded faces, all alive,
Eyes, of their own lids flashing themselves bare,
   And brows that with a mobile life contrive
A deeper shadow, – may we in no wise dare
   To put a finger out, and touch a man,   800
And cry 'this is the leader?' What, all these! –
   Broad heads, black eyes, – yet not a soul that ran
From God down with a message? all, to please
   The donna waving measures with her fan,
And not the judgment-angel on his knees,
   (The trumpet just an inch off from his lips)
Who when he breathes next, will put out the sun?

   Yet mankind's self were foundered in eclipse,
If lacking doers, with great works to be done;
   And lo, the startled earth already dips   810
Back into light – a better day's begun –

And soon this leader, teacher, will stand plain,
And build the golden pipes and synthesize
   This people-organ for a holy strain.
We hold this hope, and still in all these eyes,
   Go sounding for the deep look which shall drain
Suffused thought into channelled enterprise.
   Where is the teacher? What now may he do,
Who shall do greatly? Doth he gird his waist
   With a monk's rope, like Luther? or pursue   820
The goat, like Tell? or dry his nets in haste,
   Like Masaniello when the sky was blue?
Keep house, like other peasants, with inlaced,
   Bare, brawny arms about a favourite child,
And meditative looks beyond the door,
   (But not to mark the kidling's teeth have filed
The green shoots of his vine which last year bore
   Full twenty bunches,) or, on triple-piled
Throne-velvets sit at ease, to bless the poor,
   Like other pontiffs, in the Poorest's name?   830
The old tiara keeps itself aslope
   Upon his steady brows, which, all the same,
Bend mildly to permit the people's hope?

Whatever hand shall grasp this oriflamme,
Whatever man (last peasant or first pope
   Seeking to free his country!) shall appear,
Teach, lead, strike fire into the masses, fill
   These empty bladders with fine air, insphere
These wills into a unity of will,
   And make of Italy a nation – dear   840
And blessed be that man! the Heavens shall kill
   No leaf the earth lets grow for him, and Death
Shall cast him back upon the lap of Life
   To live more surely, in a clarion-breath
Of hero-music. Brutus, with the knife,
   Rienzi, with the fasces, throb beneath
Rome's stones, – and more, – who threw away joy's fife
   Like Pallas, that the beauty of their souls
Might ever shine untroubled and entire.
   But if it can be true that he who rolls   850

The Church's thunders, will reserve her fire
   For only light, – from eucharistic bowls
Will pour new life for nations that expire,
   And rend the scarlet of his papal vest
To gird the weak loins of his countrymen –
   I hold that he surpasses all the rest
Of Romans, heroes, patriots, – and that when
   He sat down on the throne, he dispossessed
The first graves of some glory. See again,
   This country-saving is a glorious thing,   860
And if a common man achieved it? well.
   Say, a rich man did? excellent. A king?
That grows sublime. A priest? improbable.
   A pope? Ah, there we stop, and cannot bring
Our faith up to the leap, with history's bell
   So heavy round the neck of it – albeit
We fain would grant the possibility,
   For *thy* sake, Pio nono!

                      Stretch thy feet
In that case – I will kiss them reverently
   As any pilgrim to the papal seat!   870
And, such proved possible, thy throne to me
   Shall seem as holy a place as Pellico's
Venetian dungeon, or as Spielberg's grate,
   At which the Lombard woman hung the rose
Of her sweet soul, by its own dewy weight,
   To feel the dungeon round her sunshine close,
And pining so, died early, yet too late
   For what she suffered. Yea, I will not choose
Betwixt thy throne, Pope Pius, and the spot
   Marked red for ever, spite of rains and dews,   880
Where two fell riddled by the Austrian's shot,
   The brothers Bandiera, who accuse,
With one same mother-voice and face (that what
   They speak may be invincible) the sins
Of earth's tormentors before God the just,
   Until the unconscious thunder-bolt begins
To loosen in His grasp.

                              And yet we must
      Beware, and mark the natural kiths and kins
Of circumstance and office, and distrust
      The rich man reasoning in a poor man's hut,   890
The poet who neglects pure truth to prove
      Statistic fact, the child who leaves a rut
For a smoother road, the priest who vows his glove
      Exhales no grace, the prince who walks-a-foot,
The woman who has sworn she will not love,
      And this Ninth Pius in Seventh Gregory's chair,
With Andrea Doria's forehead!

                              Count what goes
      To making up a pope, before he wear
That triple crown. We pass the world-wide throes
      Which went to make the popedom, – the despair   900
Of free men, good men, wise men; the dread shows
      Of women's faces, by the faggot's flash,
Tossed out, to the minutest stir and throb
      O' the white lips, the least tremble of a lash,
      To glut the red stare of a licensed mob;
      The short mad cries down oubliettes, and plash
So horribly far off; priests, trained to rob,
      And kings that, like encouraged nightmares, sate
On nation's hearts most heavily distressed
      With monstrous sights and apophthegms of fate! –   910
We pass these things, – because 'the times' are prest
      With necessary charges of the weight
Of all this sin, and 'Calvin, for the rest,
      Made bold to burn Servetus – Ah, men err!' –
And, so do *churches!* which is all we mean
      To bring to proof in any register
Of theological fat kine and lean –
      So drive them back into the pens! refer
Old sins (with pourpoint, 'quotha' and 'I ween,')
      Entirely to the old times, the old times;   920
Nor ever ask why this preponderant,
      Infallable, pure Church could set her chimes
Most loudly then, just then, – most jubilant,
      Precisely then – when mankind stood in crimes

Full heart-deep, and Heaven's judgments were not scant.
   Inquire still less, what signifies a church
Of perfect inspiration and pure laws,
   Who burns the first man with a brimstone-torch,
And grinds the second, bone by bone, because
   The times, forsooth, are used to rack and scorch!   930
What *is* a holy Church, unless she awes
   The times down from their sins? Did Christ select
Such amiable times, to come and teach
   Love to, and mercy? The whole world we wrecked,
If every mere great man, who lives to reach
   A little leaf of popular respect,
Attained not simply by some special breach
   In the age's customs, by some precedence
In thought and act, which, having proved him higher
   Than those he lived with, proved his competence   940
In helping them to wonder and aspire.

   My words are guiltless of the bigot's sense.
My soul has fire to mingle with the fire
   Of all these souls, within or out of doors
Of Rome's church or another. I believe
   In one Priest, and one temple, with its floors
Of shining jasper gloom'd at morn and eve
   By countless knees of earnest auditors,
And crystal walls, too lucid to perceive,
   That none may take the measure of the place   950
And say, 'So far the porphyry, then, the flint –
   To this mark, mercy goes, and there, ends grace,'
Though still the permeable crystals hint
   At some white starry distance, bathed in space.
I feel how nature's ice-crusts keep the dint
   Of undersprings of silent Deity.
I hold the articulated gospels, which
   Show Christ among us, crucified on tree.
I love all who love truth, if poor or rich
   In what they have won of truth possessively.   960
No altars and no hands defiled with pitch
   Shall scare me off, but I will pray and eat
With all these – taking leave to choose my ewers

And say at last, 'Your visible churches cheat
Their inward types, – and, if a church assures
    Of standing without failure and defeat,
The same both fails and lies.'

                                        To leave which lures
    Of wider subject through past years, – behold,
We come back from the popedom to the pope,
    To ponder what he *must* be, ere we are bold   970
For what he *may* be, with our heavy hope
    To trust upon his soul. So, fold by fold,
Explore this mummy in the priestly cope,
    Transmitted through the darks of time, to catch
The man within the wrappage, and discern
    How he, an honest man, upon the watch
Full fifty years, for what a man may learn,
    Contrived to get just there; with what a snatch
Of old-world oboli he had to earn
    The passage through; with what a drowsy sop,   980
To drench the busy barkings of his brain;
    What ghosts of pale tradition, wreathed with hop
'Gainst wakeful thought, he had to entertain
    For heavenly visions; and consent to stop
The clock at noon, and let the hour remain
    (Without vain windings up) inviolate,
Against all chimings from the belfry. Lo,
    From every given pope you must abate,
Albeit you love him, some things – good, you know –
    Which every given heretic you hate,   990
Assumes for his, as being plainly so.
    A pope must hold by popes a little, – yes,
By councils, – from Nicæa up to Trent, –
    By hierocratic empire, more or less
Irresponsible to men, – he must resent
    Each man's particular conscience, and repress
Inquiry, meditation, argument,
    As tyrants faction. Also, he must not
Love truth too dangerously, but prefer
    'The interests of the Church,' (because a blot   1000
Is better than a rent, in miniver)

Submit to see the people swallow hot
Husk-porridge, which his chartered churchmen stir
   Quoting the only one true God's epigraph,
'Feed my lambs, Peter!' – must consent to sit
   Attesting with his pastoral ring and staff,
To such a picture of our Lady, hit
   Off well by artist angels, (though not half
As fair as Giotto would have painted it) –
   To such a vial, where a dead man's blood   1010
Runs yearly warm beneath a churchman's finger;
   To such a holy house of stone and wood,
Whereof a cloud of angels was the bringer
   From Bethlehem to Loreto. – Were it good
For any pope on earth to be a flinger
   Of stones against these high-niched counterfeits?
Apostrates only are iconoclasts.
   He dares not say, while this false thing abets
That true thing, 'this is false.' He keeps his fasts
   And prayers, as prayer and fast were silver frets   1020
To change a note upon a string that lasts,
   And make a lie a virtue. Now, if he
Did more than this, higher hoped, and braver dared,
   I think he were a pope in jeopardy,
Or no pope rather, for his truth had barred
   The vaulting of his life, – and certainly,
If he do only this, mankind's regard
   Moves on from him at once, to seek some new
Teacher and leader. He is good and great
   According to the deeds a pope can do;   1030
Most liberal, save those bonds; affectionate,
   As princes may be, and, as priests are, true;
But only the ninth Pius after eight,
   When all's praised most. At best and hopefullest,
He's pope – we want a man! his heart beats warm,
   But, like the prince enchanted to the waist,
He sits in stone, and hardens by a charm
   Into the marble of his throne high-placed.
Mild benediction, waves his saintly arm –
   So, good! but what we want's a perfect man,   1040
Complete and all alive: half travertine

Half suits our need, and ill subserves our plan.
Feet, knees, nerves, sinews, energies divine
   Were never yet too much for men who ran
In such hard ways as must be this of thine,
   Deliverer whom we seek, whoe'er thou art,
Pope, prince, or peasant! If, indeed, the first,
   The noblest, therefore! since the heroic heart
Within thee must be great enough to burst
   Those trammels buckling to the baser part   1050
Thy saintly peers in Rome, who crossed and cursed
   With the same finger.

                    Come, appear, be found,
If pope or peasant, come! we hear the cock,
   The courtier of the mountains when first crowned
With golden dawn; and orient glories flock
   To meet the sun upon the highest ground.
Take voice and work! we wait to hear thee knock
   At some one of our Florentine nine gates,
On each of which was imaged a sublime
   Face of a Tuscan genius, which, for hate's   1060
And love's sake, both, our Florence in her prime
   Turned boldly on all comers to her states,
As heroes turned their shields in antique time,
   Emblazoned with honourable acts. And though
The gates are blank now of such images,
   And Petrarch looks no more from Nicolo
Toward dear Arezzo, 'twixt the acacia trees,
   Nor Dante, from gate Gallo – still we know,
Despite the razing of the blazonries,
   Remains the consecration of the shield!   1070
The dead heroic faces will start out
   On all these gates, if foes should take the field,
And blend sublimely, at the earliest shout,
   With living heroes who will scorn to yield
A hair's-breadth even, when gazing round about,
   They find in what a glorious company
They fight the foes of Florence. Who will grudge
   His one poor life, when that great man we see
Has given five hundred years, the world being judge,

To help the glory of his Italy?   1080
Who, born the fair side of the Alps, will budge,
    When Dante stays, when Ariosto stays,
When Petrarch stays for ever? Ye bring swords,
    My Tuscans? Ay, if wanted in this haze,
Bring swords. But first bring souls! – bring thoughts and words,
    Unrusted by a tear of yesterday's,
Yet awful by its wrong, – and cut these cords,
    And mow this green lush falseness to the roots,
And shut the mouth of hell below the swathe!
    And, if ye can bring songs too, let the lute's   1090
Recoverable music softly bathe
    Some poet's hand, that, through all bursts and bruits
Of popular passion, all unripe and rathe
    Convictions of the popular intellect,
Ye may not lack a finger up the air,
    Annunciative, reproving, pure, erect,
To show which way your first Ideal bare
    The whiteness of its wings, when (sorely pecked
By falcons on your wrists) it unaware
    Arose up overhead, and out of sight.   1100

Meanwhile, let all the far ends of the world
    Breathe back the deep breath of their old delight,
To swell the Italian banner just unfurled.
    Help, lands of Europe! for, if Austria fight,
The drums will bar your slumber. Had ye curled
    The laurel for your thousand artists' brows,
If these Italian hands had planted none?
    Can any sit down idle in the house,
Nor hear appeals from Buonarroti's stone
    And Raffael's canvas, rousing and to rouse?   1110
Where's Poussin's master? Gallic Avignon
    Bred Laura, and Vaucluse's fount has stirred
The heart of France too strongly, as it lets
    Its little stream out, (like a wizard's bird
Which bounds upon its emerald wing and wets
    The rocks on each side) that she should not gird
Her loins with Charlemagne's sword when foes beset
    The country of her Petrarch. Spain may well

Be minded how from Italy she caught,
    To mingle with her tinkling Moorish bell,   1120
A fuller cadence and a subtler thought.
    And even the New World, the receptacle
Of freemen, may send glad men, as it ought,
    To greet Vespucci Amerigo's door.
While England claims, by trump of poetry,
    Verona, Venice, the Ravenna-shore,
And dearer holds John Milton's Fiesole
    Than Langlande's Malvern with the stars in flower.

And Vallombrosa, we two went to see
    Last June, beloved companion, – where sublime   1130
The mountains live in holy families,
    And the slow pinewoods ever climb and climb
Half up their breasts, just stagger as they seize
    Some grey crag, drop back with it many a time,
And straggle blindly down the precipice!
    The Vallombrosan brooks were strewn as thick
That June-day, knee-deep, with dead beechen leaves,
    As Milton saw them, ere his heart grew sick
And his eyes blind. I think the monks and beeves
    Are all the same too. Scarce they have changed the wick   1140
On good St Gaulbert's altar, which receives
    The convent's pilgrims, – and the pool in front
(Wherein the hill-stream trout are cast, to wait
    The beatific vision and the grunt
Used at refectory) keeps its weedy state,
    To baffle saintly abbots who would count
The fish across their breviary nor 'bate
    The measure of their steps. O waterfalls
And forests! sound and silence! mountains bare,
    That leap up peak by peak, and catch the palls   1150
Of purple and silver mist to rend and share
    With one another, at electric calls
Of life in the sunbeams, – till we cannot dare
    Fix your shapes, count your number! we must think
Your beauty and your glory helped to fill
    The cup of Milton's souls so to the brink,
He never more was thirsty, when God's will
    Had shattered to his sense the last chain-link

By which he had drawn from Nature's visible
    The fresh well-water. Satisfied by this,   1160
He sang of Adam's paradise and smiled,
    Remembering Vallombrosa. Therefore is
The place divine to English man and child,
    And pilgrims leave their souls here in a kiss.

For Italy's the whole earth's treasury, piled
    With reveries of gentle ladies, flung
Aside, like ravelled silk, from life's worn stuff;
    With coins of scholars' fancy, which, being rung
On work-day counter, still sound silver-proof;
    In short, with all the dreams of dreamers young,   1170
Before their heads have time for slipping off
    Hope's pillow to the ground. How oft, indeed,
We've sent our souls out from the rigid north,
    On bare white feet which would not print nor bleed,
To climb the Alpine passes and look forth,
    Where booming low the Lombard rivers lead
To gardens, vineyards, all a dream is worth, –
    Sights, thou and I, Love, have seen afterward
From Tuscan Bellosguardo, wide awake,
    When, standing on the actual blessed sward   1180
Where Galileo stood at nights to take
    The vision of the stars, we have found it hard,
Gazing upon the earth and heaven, to make
    A choice of beauty.

                    Therefore let us all
Refreshed in England or in other land,
    By visions, with their fountain-rise and fall,
Of this earth's darling, – we, who understand
    A little how the Tuscan musical
Vowels do round themselves as if they planned
    Eternities of separate sweetness, – we,   1190
Who loved Sorrento vines in picture-book,
    Or ere in wine-cup we pledged faith or glee, –
Who loved Rome's wolf, with demi-gods at suck,
    Or ere we loved truth's own divinity, –
Who loved, in brief, the classic hill and brook,

And Ovid's dreaming tales, and Petrarch's song,
Or ere we loved Love's self even! – let us give
    The blessing of our souls, (and wish them strong
To bear it to the height where prayers arrive,
    When faithful spirits pray against a wrong,)   1200
To this great cause of southern men, who strive
    In God's name for man's rights, and shall not fail!

Behold, they shall not fail. The shouts ascend
    Above the shrieks, in Naples, and prevail.
Rows of shot corpses, waiting for the end
    Of burial, seem to smile up straight and pale
Into the azure air and apprehend
    That final gun-flash from Palermo's coast
Which lightens their apocalypse of death.
    So let them die! The world shows nothing lost;   1210
Therefore, not blood. Above or underneath,
    What matter, brothers, if ye keep your post
On duty's side? As sword returns to sheath,
    So dust to grave, but souls find place in Heaven.
Heroic daring is the true success,
    The eucharistic bread requires no leaven;
And though your ends were hopeless, we should bless
    Your cause as holy. Strive – and, having striven,
Take, for God's recompense, that righteousness!

From *Aurora Leigh*

Aurora Leigh is the daughter of an English father and an Italian
mother. Her mother having died when Aurora was four years old,
Aurora is brought up by her father in Italy. Her father dies when
she is thirteen and Aurora moves to England. Her father's sister
becomes her guardian, and tries to educate Aurora in the manner
of the English gentry. Aurora is both self-conscious about and
resistant to the forms of education favoured by her aunt and uses
her father's library secretly to give herself an alternative education.

At the age of twenty her cousin, Romney Leigh, proposes to her, asking her to abandon her poetic and intellectual enterprises and to aid him in his quest for social and political reforms. Aurora refuses Romney's proposal to the anger of her aunt. When her aunt dies Aurora is left with only £300 – marriage to Romney would have guaranteed her financial security.

Aurora moves to London and attempts to make a living as a writer. Romney, meanwhile, continues his philanthropic adventures, during which he rescues and gets employment for Marian Erle, a working-class girl who has run away from violent parents. Having been refused by Aurora, Romney decides to marry for principles rather than love and proposes to Marian. Aurora is informed of the proposed marriage by Lady Waldemar, who is also in love with Romney and who believes that Aurora will be able to stop the marriage. Aurora, however, does not attempt to prevent Romney marrying, though on the wedding day Romney is left standing at the altar, receiving a letter from Marian explaining that she could not marry someone who did not love her.

Aurora, on a trip to the continent, sees Marian, who now has a son. Marian reveals that Lady Waldemar persuaded her not to marry Romney and that after arriving in France (with the 'help' of Lady Waldemar) she was deserted and later raped. Aurora and Marian go to Florence together to bring up Marian's child, Aurora believing that Romney has married Lady Waldemar. Aurora hears from England that Romney has been ill, and when he arrives in Florence, it transpires that he has not married at all, and that he is still willing to marry Marian (though she will now not marry him). Romney has been blinded during a riot at Leigh Hall and has decided to turn away from his philanthropy. His blindness leads him to review Aurora's profession as a poet, and they confess their love for each other.

[FIRST BOOK, ll. 1–64]

Of writing many books there is no end;
And I who have written much in prose and verse
For others' uses, will write now for mine, –
Will write my story for my better self,
As when you paint your portrait for a friend,
Who keeps it in a drawer and looks at it
Long after he has ceased to love you, just

To hold together what he was and is.
I, writing thus, am still what men call young;
I have not so far left the coasts of life   10
To travel inland, that I cannot hear
That murmur of the outer Infinite
Which unweaned babies smile at in their sleep
When wondered at for smiling; not so far,
But still I catch my mother at her post
Beside the nursery door, with finger up,
'Hush, hush – here's too much noise!' while her sweet eyes
Leap forward, taking part against her word
In the child's riot. Still I sit and feel
My father's slow hand, when she had left us both,   20
Stroke out my childish curls across his knee,
And hear Assunta's daily jest (she knew
He liked it better than a better jest)
Inquire how many golden scudi went
To make such ringlets. O my father's hand,
Stroke heavily, heavily the poor hair down,
Draw, press the child's head closer to thy knee!
I'm still too young, too young, to sit alone.
I write. My mother was a Florentine,
Whose rare blue eyes were shut from seeing me   30
When scarcely I was four years old, my life
A poor spark snatched up from a failing lamp
Which went out therefore. She was weak and frail;
She could not bear the joy of giving life,
The mother's rapture slew her. If her kiss
Had left a longer weight upon my lips
It might have steadied the uneasy breath,
And reconciled and fraternised my soul
With the new order. As it was, indeed,
I felt a mother-want about the world,   40
And still went seeking, like a bleating lamb
Left out at night in shutting up the fold, –
As restless as a nest-deserted bird
Grown chill through something being away, though what
It knows not. I, Aurora Leigh, was born
To make my father sadder, and myself
Not overjoyous, truly. Women know

The way to rear up children (to be just),
They know a simple, merry, tender knack
Of tying sashes, fitting baby-shoes,   50
And stringing pretty words that make no sense,
And kissing full sense into empty words,
Which things are corals to cut life upon,
Although such trifles: children learn by such,
Love's holy earnest in a pretty play
And get not over-early solemnised,
But seeing, as in a rose-bush, Love's Divine
Which burns and hurts not, – not a single bloom, –
Become aware and unafraid of Love.
Such good do mothers. Fathers love as well   60
– Mine did, I know, – but still with heavier brains,
And wills more consciously responsible,
And not as wisely, since less foolishly;
So mothers have God's license to be missed.

[FIRST BOOK, ll. 135–215]

                    I, a little child, would crouch
For hours upon the floor with knees drawn up,
And gaze across them, half in terror, half
In adoration, at the picture there, –
That swan-like supernatural white life
Just sailing upward from the red stiff silk   70
Which seemed to have no part in it nor power
To keep it from quite breaking out of bounds.
For hours I sat and stared. Assunta's awe
And my poor father's melancholy eyes
Still pointed that way. That way went my thoughts
When wandering beyond sight. And as I grew
In years, I mixed, confused, unconsciously,
Whatever I last read or heard or dreamed,
Abhorrent, admirable, beautiful,
Pathetical, or ghastly, or grotesque,   80
With still that face . . . which did not therefore change,
But kept the mystic level of all forms,
Hates, fears, and admirations, was by turns
Ghost, fiend, and angel, fairy, witch, and sprite,
A dauntless Muse who eyes a dreadful Fate,

A loving Psyche who loses sight of Love,
A still Medusa with mild milky brows
All curdled and all clothed upon with snakes
Whose slime falls fast as sweat will; or anon
Our Lady of the Passion, stabbed with swords   90
Where the Babe sucked; or Lamia in her first
Moonlighted pallor, ere she shrunk and blinked
And shuddering wriggled down to the unclean;
Or my own mother, leaving her last smile
In her last kiss upon the baby-mouth
My father pushed down on the bed for that, –
Or my dead mother, without smile or kiss,
Buried at Florence. All which images,
Concentrated on the picture, glassed themselves
Before my meditative childhood, as   100
The incoherencies of change and death
Are represented fully, mixed and merged,
In the smooth fair mystery of perpetual Life.
And while I stared away my childish wits
Upon my mother's picture (ah, poor child!),
My father, who through love had suddenly
Thrown off the old conventions, broken loose
From chin-bands of the soul, like Lazarus,
Yet had no time to learn to talk and walk
Or grow anew familiar with the sun, –   110
Who had reached to freedom, not to action, lived,
But lived as one entranced, with thoughts, not aims, –
Whom love had unmade from a common man
But not completed to an uncommon man, –
My father taught me what he had learnt the best
Before he died and left me, – grief and love.
And, seeing we had books among the hills,
Strong words of counselling souls confederate
With vocal pines and waters, – out of books
He taught me all the ignorance of men,   120
And how God laughs in heaven when any man
Says 'Here I'm learned; this, I understand;
In that, I am never caught at fault or doubt.'
He sent the schools to school, demonstrating
A fool will pass for such through one mistake,

While a philosopher will pass for such,
Through said mistakes being ventured in the gross
And heaped up to a system.
                                    I am like,
They tell me, my dear father. Broader brows
Howbeit, upon a slenderer undergrowth   130
Of delicate features, – paler, near as grave;
But then my mother's smile breaks up the whole,
And makes it better sometimes than itself.
So, nine full years, our days were hid with God
Among his mountains: I was just thirteen,
Still growing like the plants from unseen roots
In tongue-tied Springs, – and suddenly awoke
To full life and life's needs and agonies
With an intense, strong, struggling heart beside
A stone-dead father. Life, struck sharp on death,   140
Makes awful lightning. His last word was 'Love –'
'Love, my child, love, love!' – (then he had done with grief)
'Love, my child.' Ere I answered he was gone,
And none was left to love in all the world.

There, ended childhood.

[FIRST BOOK, ll. 385–465]

                                    So it was.
I broke the copious curls upon my head
In braids, because she liked smooth-ordered hair.
I left off saying my sweet Tuscan words
Which still at any stirring of the heart   150
Came up to float across the English phrase
As lilies (*Bene* or *Che che*), because
She liked my father's child to speak his tongue.
I learnt the collects and the catechism,
The creeds, from Athanasius back to Nice,
The Articles, the Tracts *against* the times
(By no means Buonaventure's 'Prick of Love'),
And various popular synopses of
Inhuman doctrines never taught by John,
Because she liked instructed piety.   160
I learnt my complement of classic French

(Kept pure of Balzac and neologism)
And German also, since she liked a range
Of liberal education, – tongues, not books.
I learnt a little algebra, a little
Of the mathematics, – brushed with extreme flounce
The circle of the sciences, because
She misliked women who are frivolous.
I learnt the royal genealogies
Of Oviedo, the internal laws   170
Of the Burmese empire, – by how many feet
Mount Chimborazo outsoars Teneriffe,
What navigable river joins itself
To Lara, and what census of the year five
Was taken at Klagenfurt, – because she liked
A general insight into useful facts.
I learnt much music, – such as would have been
As quite impossible in Johnson's day
As still it might be wished – fine sleights of hand
And unimagined fingering, shuffling off   180
The hearer's soul through hurricanes of notes
To a noisy Tophet; and I drew . . . costumes
From French engravings, nereids neatly draped
(With smirks of simmering godship): I washed in
Landscapes from nature (rather say, washed out).
I danced the polka and Cellarius,
Spun glass, stuffed birds, and modelled flowers in wax,
Because she liked accomplishments in girls.
I read a score of books on womanhood
To prove, if women do not think at all,   190
They may teach thinking (to a maiden aunt
Or else the author), – books that boldly assert
Their right of comprehending husband's talk
When not too deep, and even of answering
With pretty 'may it please you,' or 'so it is,' –
Their rapid insight and fine aptitude,
Particular worth and general missionariness,
As long as they keep quiet by the fire
And never say 'no' when the world says 'ay,'
For that is fatal, – their angelic reach   200
Of virtue, chiefly used to sit and darn,

And fatten household sinners, – their, in brief,
Potential faculty in everything
Of abdicating power in it: she owned
She liked a woman to be womanly,
And English women, she thanked God and sighed
(Some people always sigh in thanking God),
Were models to the universe. And last
I learnt cross-stitch, because she did not like
To see me wear the night with empty hands   210
A-doing nothing. So, my shepherdess
Was something after all (the pastoral saints
Be praised for't), leaning lovelorn with pink eyes
To match her shoes, when I mistook the silks;
Her head uncrushed by that round weight of hat
So strangely similar to the tortoise-shell
Which slew the tragic-poet.
                              By the way,
The works of women are symbolical.
We sew, sew, prick our fingers, dull our sight,
Producing what? A pair of slippers, sir,   220
To put on when you're weary – or a stool
To stumble over and vex you . . . 'curse that stool!'
Or else at best, a cushion, where you lean
And sleep, and dream of something we are not
But would be for your sake. Alas, alas!
This hurts most, this – that, after all, we are paid
The worth of our work, perhaps.

[FIRST BOOK, ll. 832–95]

                    Books, books, books!
I had found the secret of a garret-room
Piled high with cases in my father's name,   230
Piled high, packed large, – where, creeping in and out
Among the giant fossils of my past,
Like some small nimble mouse between the ribs
Of a mastodon, I nibbled here and there
At this or that box, pulling through the gap,
In heats of terror, haste, victorious joy,
The first book first. And how I felt it beat
Under my pillow, in the morning's dark,

An hour before the sun would let me read!
My books! At last because the time was ripe,   240
I chanced upon the poets.
                    As the earth
Plunges in fury, when the internal fires
Have reached and pricked her heart, and, throwing flat
The marts and temples, the triumphal gates
And towers of observation, clears herself
To elemental freedom – thus, my soul,
At poetry's divine first finger-touch,
Let go conventions and sprang up surprised,
Convicted of the great eternities
Before two worlds.
                    What's this, Aurora Leigh,   250
You write so of the poets, and not laugh?
Those virtuous liars, dreamers after dark,
Exaggerators of the sun and moon,
And soothsayers in a tea-cup?
                    I write so
Of the only truth-tellers now left to God,
The only speakers of essential truth,
Opposed to relative, comparative,
And temporal truths; the only holders by
His sun-skirts, through conventional gray glooms;
The only teachers who instruct mankind   260
From just a shadow on a charnel-wall
To find man's veritable stature out
Erect, sublime, – the measure of a man,
And that's the measure of an angel, says
The apostle. Ay, and while your common men
Lay telegraphs, gauge railroads, reign, reap, dine,
And dust the flaunty carpets of the world
For kings to walk on, or our president,
The poet suddenly will catch them up
With his voice like a thunder, – 'This is soul,   270
This is life, this word is being said in heaven,
Here's God down on us! what are you about?'
How all those workers start amid their work,
Look round, look up, and feel, a moment's space,
That carpet-dusting, though a pretty trade,

Is not the imperative labour after all.

My own best poets, am I one with you,
That thus I love you, – or but one through love?
Does all this smell of thyme about my feet
Conclude my visit to your holy hill   280
In personal presence, or but testify
The rustling of your vesture through my dreams
With influent odours? When my joy and pain,
My thought and aspiration, like the stops
Of pipe or flute, are absolutely dumb
Unless melodious, do you play on me
My pipers, – and if, sooth, you did not blow,
Would no sound come? or is the music mine,
As a man's voice or breath is called his own,
Inbreathed by the Life-breather? There's a doubt   290
For cloudy seasons!

[SECOND BOOK, ll. 323–67]

                    Then I spoke.
I have not stood long on the strand of life,
And these salt waters have had scarcely time
To creep so high up as to wet my feet:
I cannot judge these tides – I shall, perhaps.
A woman's always younger than a man
At equal years, because she is disallowed
Maturing by the outdoor sun and air,
And kept in long-clothes past the age to walk.   300
Ah well, I know you men judge otherwise!
You think a woman ripens, as a peach,
In the cheeks chiefly. Pass it to me now;
I'm young in age, and younger still, I think,
As a woman. But a child may say amen
To a bishop's prayer and feel the way it goes,
And I, incapable to loose the knot
Of social questions, can approve, applaud
August compassion, Christian thoughts that shoot
Beyond the vulgar white of personal aims.   310
Accept my reverence.'
                    There he glowed on me

With all his face and eyes. 'No other help?'
Said he – 'no more than so?'
                              'What help?' I asked.
'You'd scorn my help, – as Nature's self, you say,
Has scorned to put her music in my mouth
Because a woman's. Do you now turn round
And ask for what a woman cannot give?'

'For what she only can, I turn and ask,'
He answered, catching up my hands in his,
And dropping on me from his high-eaved brow   320
The full weight of his soul, – 'I ask for love,
And that, she can; for life in fellowship
Through bitter duties – that, I know she can;
For wifehood – will she?'
                          'Now,' I said, 'may God
Be witness 'twixt us two!' and with the word,
Meseemed I floated into a sudden light
Above his stature, – 'am I proved too weak
To stand alone, yet strong enough to bear
Such leaners on my shoulder? poor to think,
Yet rich enough to sympathise with thought?   330
Incompetent to sing, as blackbirds can,
Yet competent to love, like HIM?'
                                  I paused;
Perhaps I darkened, as the lighthouse will
That turns upon the sea. 'It's always so.
Anything goes for a wife.'

                    [THIRD BOOK, ll. 758–826]

                    Two hours afterward,
Within Saint Margaret's Court I stood alone,
Close-veiled. A sick child, from an ague-fit,
Whose wasted right hand gambled 'gainst his left
With an old brass button in a blot of sun,   340
Jeered weakly at me as I passed across
The uneven pavement; while a woman, rouged
Upon the angular cheek-bones, kerchief torn,
Thin dangling locks, and flat lascivious mouth,
Cursed at a window both ways, in and out,

By turns some bed-rid creature and myself, –
'Lie still there, mother! liker the dead dog
You'll be to-morrow. What, we pick our way,
Fine madam, with those damnable small feet!
We cover up our face from doing good,   350
As if it were our purse! What brings you here,
My lady? Is't to find my gentleman
Who visits his tame pigeon in the eaves?
Our cholera catch you with its cramps and spasms,
And tumble up your good clothes, veil and all,
And turn your whiteness dead-blue.' I looked up;
I think I could have walked through hell that day,
And never flinched. 'The dear Christ comfort you,'
I said, 'you must have been most miserable
To be so cruel,' – and I emptied out   360
My purse upon the stones: when, as I had cast
The last charm in the cauldron, the whole court
Went boiling, bubbling up, from all its doors
And windows, with a hideous wail of laughs
And roar of oaths, and blows perhaps . . . I passed
Too quickly for distinguishing . . . and pushed
A little side-door hanging on a hinge,
And plunged into the dark, and groped and climbed
The long, steep, narrow stair 'twixt broken rail
And mildewed wall that let the plaster drop   370
To startle me in the blackness. Still, up, up!
So high lived Romney's bride. I paused at last
Before a low door in the roof, and knocked.
There came an answer like a hurried dove –
'So soon? can that be Mister Leigh? so soon?'
And, as I entered, an ineffable face
Met mine upon the threshold. 'Oh, not you,
Not you!' – the dropping of the voice implied;
'Then, if not you, for me not any one.'
I looked her in the eyes, and held her hands,   380
And said 'I am his cousin, – Romney Leigh's;
And here I come to see my cousin too.'
She touched me with her face and with her voice,
This daughter of the people. Such soft flowers
From such rough roots? The people, under there,

Can sin so, curse so, look so, smell so . . . faugh!
Yet have such daughters?
                              Nowise beautiful
Was Marian Erle. She was not white nor brown,
But could look either, like a mist that changed
According to being shone on more or less: 390
The hair, too, ran its opulence of curls
In doubt 'twixt dark and bright, nor left you clear
To name the colour. Too much hair perhaps
(I'll name a fault here) for so small a head,
Which seemed to droop in that side and on this,
As a full-blown rose uneasy with its weight
Though not a wind should trouble it. Again,
The dimple in the cheek had better gone
With redder, fuller rounds; and somewhat large
The mouth was, though the milky little teeth   400
Dissolved it to so infantine a smile.
For soon it smiled at me; the eyes smiled too,
But 'twas as if remembering they had wept,
And knowing they should, some day, weep again.

                      [FIFTH BOOK, ll. 1–73]

Aurora Leigh, be humble. Shall I hope
To speak my poems in mysterious tune
With man and nature? – with the lava-lymph
That trickles from successive galaxies
Still drop by drop adown the finger of God
In still new worlds? – with summer-days in this   410
That scarce dare breathe they are so beautiful?
With spring's delicious trouble in the ground,
Tormented by the quickened blood of roots,
And softly pricked by golden crocus-sheaves
In token of the harvest-time of flowers?
With winters and with autumns, – and beyond
With the human heart's large seasons, when it hopes
And fears, joys, grieves, and loves? – with all that strain
Of sexual passion, which devours the flesh
In a sacrament of souls? with mother's breasts   420
Which, round the new-made creatures hanging there,

Throb luminous and harmonious like pure spheres? –
With multitudinous life, and finally
With the great escapings of ecstatic souls,
Who, in a rush of too long prisoned flame,
Their radiant faces upward, burn away
This dark of the body, issuing on a world
Beyond our mortal? – can I speak my verse
So plainly in tune to these things and the rest
That men shall feel it catch them on the quick   430
As having the same warrant over them
To hold and move them if they will or no,
Alike imperious as the primal rhythm
Of that theurgic nature? – I must fail,
Who fail at the beginning to hold and move
One man, – and he my cousin, and he my friend,
And he born tender, made intelligent,
Inclined to ponder the precipitous sides
Of difficult questions; yet, obtuse to *me*,
Of *me*, incurious! likes me very well,   440
And wishes me a paradise of good,
Good looks, good means, and good digestion, – ay,
But otherwise evades me, puts me off
With kindness, with a tolerant gentleness, –
Too light a book for a grave man's reading! Go,
Aurora Leigh: be humble.
                              There it is,
We women are too apt to look to one,
Which proves a certain impotence in art.
We strain our natures at doing something great,
Far less because it's something great to do,   450
Than haply that we, so, commend ourselves
As being not small, and more appreciable
To some one friend. We must have mediators
Betwixt our highest conscience and the judge;
Some sweet saint's blood must quicken in our palms,
Or all the life in heaven seems slow and cold:
Good only being perceived as the end of good,
And God alone pleased, – that's too poor, we think,
And not enough for us by any means.
Ay – Romney, I remember, told me once   460
We miss the abstract when we comprehend.

We miss it most when we aspire, – and fail.

Yet, so, I will not. – This vile woman's way
Of trailing garments shall not trip me up:
I'll have no traffic with the personal thought
In Art's pure temple. Must I work in vain,
Without the approbation of a man?
It cannot be; it shall not. Fame itself,
That approbation of the general race,
Presents a poor end (though the arrow speed   470
Shot straight with vigorous finger to the white),
And the highest fame was never reached except
By what was aimed above it. Art for art,
And good for God Himself, the essential Good!
We'll keep our aims sublime, our eyes erect,
Although our woman-hands should shake and fail;
And if we fail . . . But must we? –
                        Shall I fail?

[SIXTH BOOK, ll. 736–93]

                'Kill! O Christ,' she said,
And turned her wild sad face from side to side   570
With most despairing wonder in it, 'What,
What have you in your souls against me then,
All of you? am I wicked, do you think?
God knows me, trusts me with the child; but you,
You think me really wicked?'
                        'Complaisant,'
I answered softly, 'to a wrong you've done,
Because of certain profits, – which is wrong
Beyond the first wrong, Marian. When you left
The pure place and the noble heart, to take
The hand of a seducer' . . .   580
                'Whom? whose hand?
I took the hand of' . . .
                . . . Springing up erect,
And lifting up the child at full arm's length,
As if to bear him like an oriflamme
Unconquerable to armies of reproach, –
'By *him*,' she said, 'my child's head and its curls,

By these blue eyes no woman born could dare
A perjury on, I make my mother's oath,
That if I left that Heart, to lighten it,
The blood of mine was still, except for grief!
No cleaner maid than I was took a step   590
To a sadder end, – no matron-mother now
Looks backward to her early maidenhood
Through chaster pulses. I speak steadily;
And if I lie so, . . . if, being fouled in will
And paltered with in soul by devil's lust,
I dared to bid this angel take my part, . . .
Would God sit quiet, let us think, in heaven,
Nor strike me dumb with thunder? Yet I speak:
He clears me therefore. What, "seduced"'s your word!
Do wolves seduce a wandering fawn in France?   600
Do eagles, who have pinched a lamb with claws,
Seduce it into carrion? So with me.
I was not ever, as you say, seduced,
But simply, murdered.'
                        There she paused, and sighed
With such a sigh as drops from agony
To exhaustion, – sighing while she let the babe
Slide down upon her bosom from her arms,
And all her face's light fell after him
Like a torch quenched in falling. Down she sank,   610
And sat upon the bedside with the child.

But I, convicted, broken utterly,
With woman's passion clung about her waist
And kissed her hair and eyes, – 'I have been wrong,
Sweet Marian' . . . (weeping in a tender rage) . . .
'Sweet holy Marian! And now, Marian, now,
I'll use your oath although my lips are hard,
And by the child, my Marian, by the child,
I swear his mother shall be innocent
Before my conscience, as in the open Book   620
Of Him who reads for judgment. Innocent,
My sister! let the night be ne'er so dark
The moon is surely somewhere in the sky;
So surely is your whiteness to be found

Through all dark facts. But pardon, pardon me,
And smile a little, Marian, – for the child,
If not for me, my sister.'

[SEVENTH BOOK, ll. 174–227]

                    It is strange,
To-day while Marian told her story like
To absorb most listeners, how I listened chief   630
To a voice not hers, nor yet that enemy's,
Nor God's in wrath, . . . but one that mixed with mine
Long years ago among the garden-trees,
And said to *me*, to *me* too, 'Be my wife,
Aurora.' It is strange with what a swell
Of yearning passion, as a snow of ghosts
Might beat against the impervious door of heaven,
I thought, 'Now, if I had been a woman, such
As God made women, to save men by love, –
By just my love I might have saved this man,   640
And made a nobler poem for the world
Than all I have failed in.' But I failed besides
In this; and now he's lost! through me alone!
And, by my only fault, his empty house
Sucks in, at this same hour, a wind from hell
To keep his hearth cold, make his casements creak
For ever to the tune of plague and sin –
O Romney, O my Romney, O my friend,
My cousin and friend! my helper, when I would,
My love, that might be! mine!
                              Why, how one weeps   650
When one's too weary! Were a witness by,
He'd say some folly . . . that I loved the man,
Who knows? . . . and make me laugh again for scorn.
At strongest, women are as weak in flesh,
As men, at weakest, vilest, are in soul:
So, hard for women to keep pace with men!
As well give up at once, sit down at once,
And weep as I do. Tears, tears! why
'Tis worth inquiry? – that we've shamed a life,
Or lost a love, or missed a world, perhaps?   660
By no means. Simply that we've walked too far,

Or talked too much, or felt the wind i' the east, –
And so we weep, as if both body and soul
Broke up in water – this way.
                              Poor mixed rags
Forsooth we're made of, like those other dolls
That lean with pretty faces into fairs.
It seems as if I had a man in me,
Despising such a woman.
                        Yet indeed,
To see a wrong or suffering moves us all
To undo it though we should undo ourselves,   670
Ay, all the more, that we undo ourselves;
That's womanly, past doubt, and not ill-moved.
A natural movement therefore, on my part,
To fill the chair up of my cousin's wife,
And save him from a devil's company!
We're all so, – made so – 'tis our woman's trade
To suffer torment for another's ease.
The world's male chivalry has perished out,
But women are knights-errant to the last;
And if Cervantes had been Shakespeare too,   680
He had made his Don a Donna.

[SEVENTH BOOK, ll. 749–94]

                    I have written truth,
And I a woman, – feebly, partially,
Inaptly in presentation, Romney'll add,
Because a woman. For the truth itself,
That's neither man's nor woman's, but just God's,
None else has reason to be proud of truth:
Himself will see it sifted, disenthralled,
And kept upon the height and in the light,
As far as and no farther than 'tis truth;   690
For, now He has left off calling firmaments
And strata, flowers and creatures, very good,
He says it still of truth, which is His own.
Truth, so far, in my book; the truth which draws
Through all things upwards – that a twofold world
Must go to a perfect cosmos. Natural things
And spiritual, – who separates those two

In art, in morals, or the social drift,
Tears up the bond of nature and brings death,
Paints futile pictures, writes unreal verse,   700
Leads vulgar days, deals ignorantly with men,
Is wrong, in short, at all points. We divide
This apple of life, and cut it through the pips:
The perfect round which fitted Venus' hand
Has perished as utterly as if we ate
Both halves. Without the spiritual, observe,
The natural's impossible – no form,
No motion: without sensuous, spiritual
Is inappreciable, – no beauty or power:
And in this twofold sphere the twofold man   710
(For still the artist is intensely a man)
Holds firmly by the natural, to reach
The spiritual beyond it, – fixes still
The type with mortal vision, to pierce through,
With eyes immortal, to the antitype
Some call the ideal, – better called the real,
And certain to be called so presently
When things shall have their names. Look long enough
On any peasant's face here, coarse and lined,
You'll catch Antinous somewhere in that clay,   720
As perfect featured as he yearns at Rome
From marble pale with beauty; then persist,
And, if your apprehension's competent,
You'll find some fairer angel at his back,
As much exceeding him as he the boor,
And pushing him with empyreal disdain
For ever out of sight.

                    [EIGHTH BOOK, ll. 261–352]

                    'I have read your book,
Aurora.'
                    'You have read it,' I replied,
'And I have writ it, – we have done with it.   730
And now the rest?'
                    'The rest is like the first,'
He answered, – 'for the book is in my heart,
Lives in me, wakes in me, and dreams in me:

My daily bread tastes of it, – and my wine
Which has no smack of it, I pour it out,
It seems unnatural drinking.'
                                        Bitterly
I took the word up; 'Never waste your wine.
The book lived in me ere it lived in you;
I know it closer than another does,
And how it's foolish, feeble, and afraid,   740
And all unworthy so much compliment.
Beseech you, keep your wine, – and, when you drink,
Still wish some happier fortune to a friend,
Than even to have written a far better book.'

He answered gently, 'That is consequent:
The poet looks beyond the book he has made,
Or else he had not made it. If a man
Could make a man, he'd henceforth be a god
In feeling what a little thing is man:
It is not my case. And this special book,   750
I did not make it, to make light of it:
It stands above my knowledge, draws me up;
'Tis high to me. It may be that the book
Is not so high, but I so low, instead;
Still high to me. I mean no compliment:
I will not say there are not, young or old,
Male writers, ay, or female, let it pass,
Who'll write us richer and completer books.
A man may love a woman perfectly,
And yet by no means ignorantly maintain   760
A thousand women have not larger eyes:
Enough that she alone has looked at him
With eyes that, large or small, have won his soul.
And so, this book, Aurora, – so, your book.'

'Alas,' I answered, 'is it so, indeed?'
And then was silent.
                    'Is it so, indeed,'
He echoed, 'that *alas* is all your word?'
I said, 'I'm thinking of a far-off June,
When you and I, upon my birthday once,
Discoursed of life and art, with both untried.   770

I'm thinking, Romney, how 'twas morning then,
And now 'tis night.'
                              'And now,' he said, 'tis night.'

'I'm thinking,' I resumed, ' 'tis somewhat sad,
That if I had known, that morning in the dew,
My cousin Romney would have said such words
On such a night at close of many years,
In speaking of a future book of mine,
It would have pleased me better as a hope,
Than as an actual grace it can at all:
That's sad, I'm thinking.'
                              'Ay,' he said, ' 'tis night.'   780

'And there,' I added lightly, 'are the stars!
And here, we'll talk of stars and not of books.'

'You have the stars,' he murmured, – 'it is well:
Be like them! shine, Aurora, on my dark,
Though high and cold and only like a star,
And for this short night only, – you, who keep
The same Aurora of the bright June-day
That withered up the flowers before my face,
And turned me from the garden evermore
Because I was not worthy. Oh, deserved,   790
Deserved! that I, who verily had not learnt
God's lesson half, attaining as a dunce
To obliterate good words with fractious thumbs
And cheat myself of the context, – I
Aside, with male ferocious impudence,
The world's Aurora who had conned her part
On the other side the leaf! ignore her so,
Because she was a woman and a queen,
And had no beard to bristle through her song,
My teacher, who has taught me with a book,   800
My Miriam, whose sweet mouth, when nearly drowned
I still heard singing on the shore! Deserved,
That here I should look up unto the stars
And miss the glory' . . .
                              'Can I understand?'

I broke in. 'You speak wildly, Romney Leigh,
Or I hear wildly. In that morning-time
We recollect, the roses were too red,
The trees too green, reproach too natural
If one should see not what the other saw:
And now, it's night, remember; we have shades   810
In place of colours; we are now grown cold,
And old, my cousin Romney. Pardon me, –
I'm very happy that you like my book,
And very sorry that I quoted back
A ten years' birthday. 'Twas so mad a thing
In any woman, I scarce marvel much
You took it for a venturous piece of spite,
Provoking such excuses as indeed
I cannot call you slack in.'

[NINTH BOOK, ll.321–452]

'. . . The truth is, I am grown so proud with grief,   820
And He has said so often through His nights
And through His mornings, "Weep a little still,
Thou foolish Marian, because women must,
But do not blush at all except for sin" –
That I, who felt myself unworthy once
Of virtuous Romney and his high-born race,
Have come to learn, – a woman, poor or rich,
Despised or honoured, is a human soul,
And what her soul is, that she is herself,
Although she should be spit upon of men,   830
As is the pavement of the churches here,
Still good enough to pray in. And being chaste
And honest, and inclined to do the right,
And love the truth, and live my life out green
And smooth beneath his steps, I should not fear
To make him thus a less uneasy time
Than many a happier woman. Very proud
You see me. Pardon, that I set a trap
To hear a confirmation in your voice,
Both yours and yours. It is so good to know   840
'Twas really God who said the same before;
And thus it is in heaven, that first God speaks,

And then His angels. Oh, it does me good,
It wipes me clean and sweet from devil's dirt,
That Romney Leigh should think me worthy still
Of being his true and honourable wife!
Henceforth I need not say, on leaving earth,
I had no glory in it. For the rest,
The reason's ready (master, angel, friend,
Be patient with me) wherefore you and I   850
Can never, never, never join hands so.
I know you'll not be angry like a man
(For *you* are none) when I shall tell the truth,
Which is, I do not love you, Romney Leigh,
I do not love you. Ah well! catch my hands,
Miss Leigh, and burn into my eyes with yours –
I swear I do not love him. Did I once?
'Tis said that woman have been bruised to death
And yet, if once they loved, that love of theirs
Could never be drained out with all their blood: 860
I've heard such things and pondered. Did I indeed
Love once; or did I only worship? Yes,
Perhaps, O friend, I set you so high
Above all actual good or hope of good
Or fear of evil, all that could be mine,
I haply set you above love itself,
And set out reach of these poor woman's arms,
Angelic Romney. What was in my thought?
To be your slave, your help, your toy, your tool.
To be your love . . . I never thought of that: 870
To give you love . . . still less. I gave you love?
I think I did not give you anything;
I was but only yours – upon my knees,
All yours, in soul and body, in head and heart,
A creature you had taken from the ground
Still crumbling through your fingers to your feet
To join the dust she came from. Did I love,
Or did I worship? judge, Aurora Leigh!
But, if indeed I loved, 'twas long ago –
So long! before the sun and moon were made,   880
Before the hells were open, – ah, before

I heard my child cry in the desert night,
And knew he had no father. It may be
I'm not as strong as other woman are,
Who, torn and crushed, are not undone from love:
It may be I am colder than the dead,
Who, being dead, love always. But for me,
Once killed, this ghost of Marian loves no more,
No more . . . except the child! . . . no more at all.
I told your cousin, sir, that I was dead;   890
And now, she thinks I'll get up from my grave,
And wear my chin-cloth for a wedding-veil,
And glide along the churchyard like a bride
While all the dead keep whispering through the withes,
'You would be better in your place with us,
You pitiful corruption!' At the thought,
The damps break out on me like leprosy
Although I'm clean. Ay, clean as Marian Erle!
As Marian Leigh, I know, I were not clean:
Nor have I so much life that I should love,   900
Except the child. Ah God! I could not bear
To see my darling on a good man's knees,
And know, by such a look, or such a sigh,
Or such a silence, that he thought sometimes,
'This child was fathered by some cursèd wretch' . . .
For, Romney, angels are less tender-wise
Than God and mothers: even *you* would think
What *we* think never. He is ours, the child;
And we would sooner vex a soul in heaven
By coupling with it the dead body's thought,   910
It left behind it in a last month's grave,
Than, in my child, see other than . . . my child.
We only never call him fatherless
Who has God and his mother. O my babe,
My pretty, pretty blossom, an ill wind
Once blew upon my breast! can any think
I'd have another – one called happier,
A fathered child, with father's love and race
That's worn as bold and open as a smile,
To vex my darling when he's asked his name   920

And has no answer? What! a happier child
Than mine, my best – who laughed so loud to-night
He could not sleep for pastime? Nay, I swear,
By life and love, that, if I lived like some,
And loved like . . . *some*, ay, loved you, Romney Leigh,
As some love (eyes that have wept so much, see clear),
I've room for no more children in my arms,
My kisses are all melted on one mouth,
I would not push my darling to a stool
To dandle babies. Here's a hand shall keep   930
For ever clean without a marriage-ring,
To tend my boy until he cease to need
One steadying finger of it, and desert
(Not miss) his mother's lap, to sit with men.
And when I miss him (not he me), I'll come
And says "Now give me some of Romney" work,
To help your outcast orphans of the world
And comfort grief with grief." For you, meantime,
Most noble Romney, wed a noble wife,
And open on each other your great souls –   940
I need not farther bless you. If I dared
But strain and touch her in her upper sphere,
And say "Come down to Romney – pay my debt!"
I should be joyful with the stream of joy
Sent through me. But the moon is in my face . . .
I dare not – through I guess the name he loves;
I'm learned with my studies of old days,
Remembering how he crushed his under-lip
When some one came and spoke, or did not come.
Aurora, I could touch her with my hand,   950
And fly because I dare not.'

[NINTH BOOK, ll.624–760]

'. . . No matter: let the truth
Stand high; Aurora must be humble: no,
My love's not pity merely. Obviously
I'm not a generous woman, never was,
Or else, of old, I had not looked so near

To weights and measures, grudging you the power
To give, as first I scorned your power to judge
For me, Aurora. I would have no gifts,
Forsooth, but God's, – and I would use *them* too   960
According to my pleasure and my choice,
As He and I were equals, you below,
Excluded from that level of interchange
Admitting benefaction. You were wrong
In much? you said so. I was wrong in most.
Oh, most! You only thought to rescue men
By half-means, half-way, seeing half their wants,
While thinking nothing of your personal gain.
But I, who saw the human nature broad
At both sides, comprehending too the soul's,   970
And all the high necessities of Art,
Betrayed the thing I saw, and wronged my own life
For which I pleaded. Passioned to exalt
The artist's instinct in me at the cost
Of putting down the woman's, I forgot
No perfect artist is developed here
From any imperfect woman. Flower from root,
And spiritual from natural, grade by grade
In all our life. A handful of the earth
To make God's image! the despised poor earth,   980
The healthy, odorous earth, – I missed with it
The divine Breath that blows the nostrils out
To ineffable inflatus, – ay, the breath
Which love is. Art is much, but Love is more.
O Art, my Art, thou'rt much, but Love is more!
Art symbolises heaven, but Love is God
And makes heaven. I, Aurora, fell from mine.
I would not be a woman like the rest,
A simple woman who believes in love
And owns the right of love because she loves,   990
And, hearing she's beloved, is satisfied
With what contents God: I must analyse,
Confront, and question; just as if a fly
Refused to warm itself in any sun
Till such was *in Leone*: I must fret,

Forsooth, because the month was only May,
Be faithless of the kind of proffered love,
And captious, lest it miss my dignity,
And scornful, that my lover sought a wife
To use . . . to use! O Romney, O my love,   1000
I am changed since then, changed wholly, – for indeed
If now you'd stoop so low to take my love
And use it roughly, without stint or spare,
As men use common things with more behind
(And, in this, ever would be more behind)
To any mean and ordinary end, –
The joy would set me like a star, in heaven,
So high up, I should shine because of height
And not of virtue. Yet in one respect,
Just one, beloved, I am in nowise changed: 1010
I love you, loved you . . . loved you first and last,
And love you on for ever. Now I know
I loved you always, Romney. She who died
Knew that, and said so; Lady Waldemar
Knows that; . . . and Marian. I had known the same,
Except that I was prouder than I knew,
And not so honest. Ay, and, as I live,
I should have died so, crushing in my hand
This rose of love, the wasp inside and all,
Ignoring ever to my soul and you   1020
Both rose and pain – except for this great loss,
This great despair – to stand before your face
And know you do not see me where I stand.
You think, perhaps, I am not changed from pride
And that I chiefly bear to say such words,
Because you cannot shame me with your eyes?
O calm, grand eyes, extinguished in a storm,
Blown out like lights o'er melancholy seas,
Though shrieked for by the shipwrecked, – O my Dark,
My Cloud, – to go before me every day   1030
While I go ever toward the wilderness, –
I would that you could see me bare to the soul!
If this be pity, 'tis so for myself,
 And not for Romney! *he* can stand alone;

A man like *him* is never overcome:
No woman like me counts him pitiable
While saints applaud him. He mistook the world;
But I mistook my own heart, and that slip
Was fatal. Romney, – will you leave me here?
So wrong, so proud, so weak, so unconsoled,   1040
So mere a woman! – and I love you so,
I love you, Romney –'
                                   Could I see his face,
I wept so? Did I drop against his breast,
Or did his arms constrain me? were my cheeks
Hot, overflooded, with my tears – or his?
And which of our two large explosive hearts
So shook me? That, I know not. There were words
That broke in utterance . . . melted, in the fire, –
Embrace, that was convulsion, . . . then a kiss
As long and silent as the ecstatic night,   1050
And deep, deep, shuddering breaths, which meant beyond
Whatever could be told by word or kiss.
But what he said . . . I have written day by day,
With somewhat even writing. Did I think
That such a passionate rain would intercept
And dash this last page? what he said, indeed,
I fain would write it down here like the rest,
To keep it in my eyes, as in my ears,
The heart's sweet scripture it be read at night
When weary, or at morning when afraid,   1060
And lean my heaviest oath on when I sweat
That, when all's done, all tried, all counted here,
All great arts, and all good philosophies,
This love just puts its hand out in a dream
And straight outstretches all things.
                                   What he said,
I fain would write. But if an angel spoke
In thunder, should we haply know much more
Than that it thundered? If a cloud came down
And wrapped us wholly, could we draw its shape,
As if on the outside and not overcome?   1070
And so he spake. His breath against my face

Confused his words, yet made them more intense
(As when the sudden finger of the wind
Will wipe a row of single city-lamps
To a pure white line of flame, more luminous
Because of obliteration), more intense,
The intimate presence carrying in itself
Complete communication, as with souls
Who, having put the body off, perceive
Through simply being. Thus, 'twas granted me   1080
To know he loved me to the depth and height
Of such large natures, ever competent,
With grand horizons by the sea or land,
To love's grand sunrise. Small spheres hold small fires,
But he loved largely, as a man can love
Who, baffled in his love, dares live his life,
Accepts the ends which God loves, for his own,
And lift a constant aspect.

[NINTH BOOK, ll. 900–64]
'. . . O poet, O my love,
Since *I* was too ambitious in my deed,   1090
And thought to distance all men in success
(Till God came on me, marked the place, and said
"Ill-doer, henceforth keep within this line,
Attempting less than others," – and I stand
And work among Christ's little ones, content),
Come thou, my compensation, my dear sight,
My morning-star, my morning, – rise and shine,
And touch my hills with radiance not their own.
Shine out for two, Aurora, and fulfil
My falling-short that must be! work for two,
As I, though thus restrained, for two, shall love!
Gaze on, with inscient vision toward the sun,
And, from his visceral heat, pluck out the roots
Of light beyond him. Art's a service, – mark:
A silver key is given to thy clasp,
And thou shalt stand unwearied, night and day,
And fix it in the hard, slow-turning wards,
To open, so, that intermediate door

Betwixt the different planes of sensuous form
And form insensuous, that inferior men   1110
May learn to feel on still through these to those,
And bless thy ministration. The world waits
For help. Beloved, let us love so well,
Our work shall still be better for our love,
And still our love be sweeter for our work,
And both commended, for the sake of each,
By all true workers and true lovers born.
Now press the clarion on thy woman's lip
(Love's holy kiss shall still keep consecrate)
And breathe thy fine keen breath along the brass,   1120
And blow all class-walls level as Jericho's
Past Jordan, – crying from the top of souls,
To souls, that, here assembled on earth's flats,
They get them to some purer eminence
Than any hitherto beheld for clouds!
What height we know not, – but the way we know,
And how by mounting ever we attain,
And so climb on. It is the hour for souls,
That bodies, leavened by the will and love,
Be lighted to redemption. The world's old,   1130
But the old world waits the time to be renewed,
Toward which, new hearts in individual growth
Must quicken, and increase to multitude
In new dynasties of the race of men;
Developed whence, shall grow spontaneously
New churches, new œconomies, new laws
Admitting freedom, new socities
Excluding falsehood: HE shall make all new.'

    My Romney! – Lifting up my hand in his,
    As wheeled by Seeing spirits toward the east,   1140
He turned instinctively, where, faint and far,
Along the tingling desert of the sky,
Beyond the circle of the conscious hills,
Were laid in jasper-stone as clear as glass
The first foundations of that new, near Day
Which should be builded out of heaven to God.

He stood a moment with erected brows,
In silence, as a creature might who gazed, –
Stood calm, and fed his blind, majestic eyes
Upon the thought of perfect noon: and when   1150
I saw his soul saw, – 'Jasper first,' I said;
'And second, sapphire; third, chalcedony;
The rest in order: – last, an amethyst.'

A Curse for a Nation

PROLOGUE

I heard an angel speak last night,
        And he said 'Write!
Write a Nation's curse for me,
And sent it over the Western Sea.'

I faltered, taking up the word:
        'Not so, my lord!
If curses must be, choose another
To send thy curse against my brother.

'For I am bound by gratitude,
        By love and blood,   10
To brothers of mine across the sea,
Who stretch out kindly hands to me.'

'Therefore,' the voice said, 'shalt thou write
        My curse to-night.
From the summits of love a curse is driven,
As lightning is from the tops of heaven.'

'Not so,' I answered. 'Evermore
        My heart is sore
For my own land's sins: for little feet
Of children bleeding along the street: 20

'For parked-up honours that gainsay
          The right of way:
For almsgiving through a door that is
Not open enough for two friends to kiss:

'For love of freedom which abates
          Beyond the Straits:
For patriot virtue starved to vice on
Self-praise, self-interest, and suspicion:

'For an oligarchic parliament,
          And bribes well-meant.   30
What curse to another land assign.
When heavy-souled for the sins of mine?'

'Therefore,' the voice said, 'shalt thou write
          My curse to-night.
Because thou hast strength to see and hate
A foul thing done *within* thy gate.'

'Not so,' I answered once again.
          'To curse, choose men.
For I, a woman, have only known
How the heart melts and the tears run down.'   40

'Therefore,' the voice said, 'shalt thou write
          My curse to-night.
Some women weep and curse, I say
(And no one marvels), night and day.

'And thou shalt take their part to-night,
          Weep and write.
A curse from the depths of womanhood
Is very salt, and bitter, and good.'

So thus I wrote, and mourned indeed,
          What all may read.   50
And thus, as was enjoined on me,
I send it over the Western Sea.

THE CURSE

1

Because ye have broken your own chain
        With the strain
Of brave men climbing a Nation's height,
Yet thence bear down with brand and thong
On souls of others, – for this wrong
        This is the curse. Write.

Because yourselves are standing straight
        In the state
Of Freedom's foremost acolyte,
Yet keep calm footing all the time
On writhing bond-slaves, – for this crime
        This is the curse. Write.

Because ye prosper in God's name,
        With a claim
To honour in the old world's sight,
Yet do the fiend's work perfectly
In strangling martyrs, – for this lie
        This is the curse. Write.

2

Ye shall watch while kings conspire
Round the people's smouldering fire,
    And, warm for your part,
Shall never dare – O shame!
To utter the thought into flame
        Which burns at your heart.
        This is the curse. Write.

Ye shall watch while nations strive
With the bloodhounds, die or survive,
    Drop faint from their jaws,
Or throttle them backward to death,
And only under your breath,
        Shall favour the cause.
        This is the curse. Write.

Ye shall watch while strong men draw
The nets of feudal law
   To strangle the weak,
And, counting the sin for a sin,
Your soul shall be sadder within
   Than the word ye shall speak.   90
          This is the curse. Write.

When good men are praying erect
That Christ may avenge His elect
   And deliver the earth,
The prayer in your ears, said low,
Shall sound like the tramp of a foe
   That's driving you forth.
          This is the curse. Write.

When wise men give you their praise,
They shall pause in the heat of the phrase,   100
   As if carried too far.
When ye boast your own charters kept true,
Ye shall blush; – for the thing which ye do
   Derives what ye are.
          This is the curse. Write.

When fools cast taunts at your gate,
Your scorn ye shall somewhat abate
   As ye look o'er the wall,
For your conscience, tradition, and name
Explode with a deadlier blame   110
   Than the worst of them all.
          This is the curse. Write.

Go, wherever ill deeds shall be done,
Go, plant your flag in the sun
   Beside the ill-doers!
And recoil from clenching the curse
Of God's witnessing Universe
   With a curse of yours.
          THIS is the curse. Write.

Mother and Poet

(TURIN, AFTER NEWS FROM GAETA, 1861)

1

Dead! One of them shot by the sea in the east,
  And one of them shot in the west by the sea.
Dead! both my boys! When you sit at the feast
  And are wanting a great song for Italy free,
        Let none look at *me*!

2

Yet I was a poetess only last year,
  And good at my art, for a woman, men said;
But *this* woman, *this*, who is agonised here,
  – The east sea and west sea rhyme on in her head
        For ever instead.   10

3

What art can a woman be good at? Oh, vain!
  What art *is* she good at, but hurting her breast
With the milk-teeth of babes, and a smile at the pain?
  Ah boys, how you hurt! you were strong as you pressed,
        And I proud, by that test.

4

What art's for a woman? To hold on her knees
  Both darlings! to feel all their arms round her throat,
Cling, strangle a little! to sew by degrees
  And 'broider the long-clothes and neat little coat;
        To dream and to doat.   20

5

To teach them . . . It stings there! *I* made them indeed
  Speak plain the word *country*. *I* taught them, no doubt,
That a country's a thing men should die for at need.
  I prated of liberty, rights, and about
        The tyrant cast out.

6

And when their eyes flashed . . . O my beautiful eyes! . . .
   I exulted; nay, let them go forth at the wheels
Of the guns, and denied not. But then the surprise
   When one sits quite alone! Then one weeps, then one
     kneels!
         God, how the house feels!   30

7

At first, happy news came, in gay letters moiled
   With my kisses, – of camp-life and glory, and how
They both loved me; and, soon coming home to be spoiled
   In return would fan off every fly from my brow
        With their green laurel-bough.

8

Then was triumph at Turin: 'Ancona was free!'
   And some one came out of the cheers in the street,
With a face pale as stone, to say something to me.
   My Guido was dead! I fell down at his feet,
      While they cheered in the street.   40

9

I bore it; friends soothed me; my grief looked sublime
   As the ransom of Italy. One boy remained
To be leant on and walked with, recalling the time
   When the first grew immortal, while both of us strained
      To the height he had gained.

10

And letters still came, shorter, sadder, more strong,
   Writ now but in one hand, 'I was not to faint, –
One loved me for two – would be with me ere long:
   And *Viva l'Italia!* – *he* died for, our saint,
      Who forbids our complaint.'   50

11

My Nanni would add, 'he was safe, and aware
   Of a presence that turned off the balls, – was imprest
It was Guido himself, who knew what I could bear,

And how 'twas impossible, quite dispossessed
  To live on for the rest.'

12

On which, without pause, up the telegraph line
  Swept smoothly the next news from Gaeta: – *Shot.*
Tell his mother. Ah, ah, 'his,' 'their' mother, – not 'mine,'
  No voice says '*My* mother' again to me. What!
      You think Guido forgot?   60

13

Are souls straight so happy that, dizzy with Heaven,
  They drop earth's affections, conceive not of woe?
I think not. Themselves were too lately forgiven
  Through THAT Love and Sorrow which reconciled so
      The Above and Below.

14

O Christ of the five wounds, who look'dst through the dark
  To the face of Thy mother! consider, I pray,
How we common mothers stand desolate, mark,
  Whose sons, not being Christs, die with eyes turned away,
      And no last word to say!   70

15

Both boys dead? but that's out of nature. We all
  Have been patriots, yet each house must always keep one.
'Twere imbecile, hewing out roads to a wall;
  And, when Italy's made, for what end is it done
      If we have not a son?

16

Ah, ah, ah! when Gaeta's taken, what then?
  When the fair wicked queen sits no more at her sport
Of the fire-balls of death crashing souls out of men?
  When the guns of Cavalli with final retort
      Have cut the game short?   80

17

When Venice and Rome keep their new jubilee,
   When your flag takes all heaven for its white, green, and
      red,
When *you* have your country from mountain to sea,
   When King Victor has Italy's crown on his head,
      (And *I* have my Dead) –

18

What then? Do not mock me. Ah, ring your bells low,
   And burn your lights faintly! *My* country is *there*,
Above the star pricked by the last peak of snow:
   My Italy's THERE, with my brave civic Pair,
      To disfranchise despair!   90

19

Forgive me. Some women bear children in strength,
   And bite back the cry of their pain in self-scorn;
But the birth-pangs of nations will wring us at length
   Into wail such as this – and we sit on forlorn
      When the man-child is born.

20

Dead! One of them shot by the sea in the east,
   And one of them shot in the west by the sea.
Both! both my boys! If in keeping the feast
   You want a great song for your Italy free,
      Let none look at *me!*   100

Notes

To My Father on His Birthday First published in *An Essay on Mind, and Other Poems* (1826). ***Causa fuit Pater his:*** 'my father was the reason for these things' (Horace, *Satires*, I.6.71). **19 sylphic:** a sylph is a mythical creature supposedly inhabiting the air. **23 Echo:** (in Greek myth) a nymph loved by Pan. She was torn apart by shepherds; fragments of her are hidden in the earth. **27 Aonian:** Aonia was a district of ancient Boeotia, containing Mount Helicon, sacred to the Muses. **44 Maecenas:** Gaius Maecenas, a Roman statesman. EBB's point of reference here is the fact that Maecenas was patron to the poets Virgil, Horace and Propertius.

A Sea-Side Meditation Published in *Prometheus Bound and Other Poems* (1833). ***Ut per aquas quae nunc rerum simulacra videmus:*** 'like the images we now see reflected by water' (Lucretius, *De Rerum Natura*, I.1060). **46 pandemonic:** a rare usage referring primarily to Milton's Pandemonium (in Hell), *Paradise Lost* I.756. **60 God's creation, man's intelligence:** again, and as with line 62, evocative of themes and language in *Paradise Lost*. **62 like the serpent, once erect as they:** also Miltonic. **64 Phylacteries:** probably used here in its meaning as a preservative against disease; though there may be a play on its connotations of religious observance. **74 Cyrene's fount:** Cyrene was a Greek colony founded *c*.630 BC. **108–9 as martyrs lie/Wheel-bound:** the origin of the wheel as a punishment lies in the story of Ixion who offended Zeus and was fixed to a burning wheel that rotated continually. **133 eterne volution:** never-ending revolution, turning. 'Eterne' is an archaic form of eternal. **137 Babel:** see Genesis 11. **142 saith a scroll Apochryphal:** the angel referred to is probably Uriel.

Man and Nature From *The Seraphim, and Other Poems* (1838). **6 bosky:** bushy. **26 horrent:** bristling; can also mean shuddering.

De Profundis Published in *Poems* (1844). This poem explores the grief which EBB felt at the death of her brother Edward Moulton-Barrett ('Bro') in 1840. **83 seraphs:** heavenly entities. **85 Ancient of Days:** a biblical name for God. See Daniel 7.9 and 22. Also William Blake's painting of the same name. **87 sovran:** sovereign.

Grief Published in *Poems*.

Tears Published in *Poems*. **4 Adam forfeited the primal lot:** through original sin.

Substitution Published in *Poems*. **8 Faunus:** a god often identified with Pan.

Catarina to Camoëns Published in *Poems*. Written in 1831 and later revised. EBB read Camoëns (1542–80, Portuguese poet) in a translation by Lord Strangford, who portrays Camoëns as the Byronic lover of Catarina, a lady of the Portuguese court. **47 unweeting:** unwitting, unknowingly. **83 angelus:** the angelus-bell. **100 gittern:** an old guitar-like instrument. **119 Miserere:** a prayer derived from the fifty-first Psalm. **153 terrene:** earthly, material.

Flush or Faunus Published in *Poems* (1850). Flush was EBB's spaniel. See Virginia Woolf's *Flush* (1933). **9 Arcadian:** Arcadia was the region where Pan (the 'goatly god') supposedly lived.

Hiram Powers' Greek Slave Published in *Poems* (1850). Hiram Powers was an American sculptor. 'The Greek Slave' was shown at the Great Exhibition in 1851. It is a nude female figure representing a Greek Christian being sold in a Turkish slave market.

The Runaway Slave at Pilgrim's Point The poem was written in response to a request by the Anti-Slavery Bazaar in Boston in 1845; the poem itself was sent in February 1847. The poem was first published in *The Liberty Bell* (1848). **2 the first white pilgrim:** where the Pilgrim Fathers landed in North America. **55 the whip-poor-will or the cat of the glen:** both presumably instruments of corporal punishment. **221 the Washington-race:** white Americans.

Sonnets from the Portuguese Published in *Poems* (1850). These are original poems rather than translations. The Brownings agreed that the title would obscure their biographical nature. The title supposedly originates in the fact that RB liked EBB's poem 'Catarina to Camoëns'.
1 Theocritus: (*c*.308–*c*.240 BC), Roman poet.
2, 5 amerce: to punish or put a penalty upon.
3, 7 gages: pledges. **13 chrism:** a sacramental anointing bowl.

9, 12 Venice glass: may refer to the glazing also known as Venice turpentine.

21, 13 iterance: repetition.

24, 1 clasping knife: a knife, the blade of which folds into its handle.

42, 1: Quoting here from her own poem 'Past and Future', which had been published in *Poems* (1844).

Casa Guidi Windows Part One (1851) The Casa Guidi in Florence was the Brownings' main home in Italy. On 12 September 1847 they watched a celebratory procession which reinforced EBB's belief in the ideals of Italian nationalism. **3 *O bella libertà, O bella!*:** O beautiful freedom, O beautiful (Ital.). **20 Filicaja:** Vincenzo da Filicaia (1642–1707), Florentine poet; his texts were read as predictions of Italian unity. **32 Cybele:** originally a mother-goddess of Anatolia, Cybele's cult was widespread in Greece and Rome. She is often associated with her young lover, Attis, and with wild nature. EBB's reference appears to be to the images of Cybele (often with attendant lion) used by her worshippers. **32 Niobe:** in mythology, daughter of Tantalus and wife of Amphion. When her children were killed by Apollo and Artemis she turned into stone on Mount Sipylon. **36 Juliet:** EBB regarded Cybele, Niobe and Shakespeare's Juliet as symptomatic of the fated feminine roles in which Italy was personified. **53 Arno:** the river on which Florence stands. **54 her bridges four:** the bridges across the Arno in Florence. **68 Giotto:** Giotto di Bondone (1267–1337), Florentine artist. His campanile of the Duomo remained unfinished at his death. **73–4 Michel's Night and Day/ And Dawn and Twilight:** statues by Michaelangelo in the Sagrestia Nuova. **76 Medicean:** of the Medicis, the once-powerful family in Florence. **81 St Lawrence:** the church of San Lorenzo in Florence. **93 Urbino:** Michaelangelo's servant. Vasari relates Michaelangelo's distress at Urbino's death. **98 Angelo:** Michaelangelo (1475–1564), painter and sculptor. **168 *Se tu men bella fossi, Italia*:** 'if only you were less beautiful, O Italy' (Ital.) **176 Virgil:** Publius Vergilius Maro (70–19 BC), Roman poet. **Cicero:** Marcus Tullius Cicero (106–43 BC), Roman orator and writer. **177 Catullus:** Gaius Valerius Catullus (*c.*84–*c.*54 BC), Roman poet. **Caesar:** Gaius Julius Caesar (102/100–44 BC), Roman politician, approvingly discussed by Cicero. **178 Boccaccio:** Giovanni Boccaccio (1313–75), Italian writer. **179 Dante:** Dante Alighieri (1265–1321), Florentine poet. **Petrarch:** Francesco Petrarch (1304–74), Italian poet. **181 Angelo:** Michaelangelo. **Raffael:** Raphael Sanzio (1483–1520), Italian painter. **Pergolese:** Giovanni Battista Pergolesi (1710–36), Italian composer. **185 chaplet's:** a chaplet is a string of beads. **186 ken:** knowledge (here, perhaps memory). **195 phylac-teries:** amulets worn against disease (also has a more specific meaning of religious texts or observances, which seems less appropriate here). **256 Savonarola:** Italian monk and patriot, burned for protesting against Papal corruption in 1498. **270 Luther:** Martin Luther (1483–1546), German leader of the Reformation. **274 cowl:** an outer robe with a hood worn by monks (sometimes refers to the hood alone). **307 Jubal:** a Biblical character, one literal meaning of the name, alluded to here, is 'trumpet'. **309 Asaph:** a Biblical character associated with music and singing. **314 Miriam clashed her cymbals:** See Exodus 15.20 'Miriam took a timbral in her hand.' **316 David's strings:** King David, the psalmist. **321 St Maria Novella:** church in Florence (see notes for lined 332 and 338 below). **322–3 Macchiavel ... One:** Niccolo Machiavelli (1469–1527), Florentine political theorist. Machiavelli records this incident in his account of the plague in Florence. **332 Cimabue's Virgin:** Giovanni Cimabue (1240–1302), artist. **338 Glad Borgo:** Vasari says that while Cimabue was painting his Virgin in St Maria Novella, King Charles of Anjou came to see him. Because of the rejoicing accompanying this visit the neighbourhood has since been known as Borgo Allegri (Joyful Quarter). **346 The Lady:** presumably Cimabue's Virgin. **346 empyreal:** heavenly, celestial. **353 Raffaelhood:** the 'realm' of Raphael. **358–63:** EBB cites his incident to illustrate how close the Italian people were to what she perceives as their culture at this time. **362–3 Giotto ... Cimabue found among the sheep:** Cimabue was said to be Giotto's teacher. **379 Margheritone:** a painter supposedly jealous of Cimabue. **390 Angelico:** Fra Angelico (1387–1455), painter. **424 Troy:** site of the siege in the *Iliad*. **425 Marathon:** a town connected to Athens (cf EBB's *Battle of Marathon*). **427 benison:** blessing. **442 lachrymals:** tears. **457 palace-Pitti:** the palace of Grand Duke Leopold II in Florence. **476 Magistracy, with insignia:** referring to the significant step taken by the Grand Duke in granting a Tuscan guard. **493 new Pope:** Pius IX. **499 'Il popolo':** the people. **505–9 Siena's she-wolf ... Arezzo's steed:** the insignia of the various Tuscan states carried in the procession which the Brownings observed from Casa Guidi, 12 September 1847. **543 charta:** granting permission to form a guard. **544 Guelf's or Ghibelline's:** ancient Florentine families. **581 Loggia:** the Loggia dei Lanzi. **582 Cellini's godlike Perseus:** a statue by Benvenuto Cellini (1500–71), in the Loggia. **586 Gorgon:** a mythical figure whose face turned people into stone (figures in the Pereus myth). **590 Brutus:** Cassius Brutus, conspirator against Julius Caesar. **591 Buonarroti:**

Michaelangelo. **601–2 stone/ Called Dante's:** a stone which EBB
assumes was a favourite resting place of Dante. **605 Brunelleschi's
church:** Filipo Brunelleschi (1373–1446), builder of the church of San
Lorenzo. **608 a banished Florentine:** while Dante was on a mission to
Rome in October 1306 the Black Guelfs took power in Florence. Dante,
sympathetic to the White Guelfs, never returned. **616 Ravenna's bones:**
Ravenna is a town on the north-east coast of Italy. The Ravennans refused
to hand Dante's body over to the Florentines. **623 Santa Croce church:**
in Florence. **633 Bargello chamber:** alludes to a fresco painting by
Giotto uncovered in the nineteenth century. **634 Beatrix:** the object of
Dante's love poetry. **661 Austrian Metternich:** Clement Van Metter-
nich-Winneburg (1773–1859), Austrian chancellor. **733 'that Achil-
lean wrath . . . heroes':** see the opening of Homer's *Iliad*. **738 Ledas:**
Leda was the daughter of Thestius and mother of Helen. Zeus, assuming the
shape of a swan, raped her. **789 Væ! meâ culpâ!':** 'Væ!' is an
exclamation of pain or dread. 'Meâ culpâ!': 'It is my fault' (Latin). **792 'suo
jure':** 'under his/her/one's own jurisdiction' (Latin). **805 donna:**
woman. **821 Tell:** the legend of William Tell is appropriate here because of
its anti-Austrian themes. **822 Masaniello:** Tommaso Aniello (1522–47),
Italian fisherman who became the leader of a revolt against Spanish rule in
Naples in 1647. **834 oriflamme:** originally the sacred banner of St
Dennis which the King of France received before setting out for war.
846 Rienzi: Nicolas di Rienzi (1313–54), Roman patriot and politician.
fasces: in Rome these were a bundle of rods carried before magistrates as a
symbol of their power. **848 Pallas:** stock epithet of the goddess Athena.
868 Pio nono!: Pope Pius IX. **872–3 Pellico's/ Venetian dungeon:**
Silvio Pellico (1788–1854), Italian dramatist, activist against Austrian
rule. He was arrested in October 1820 and imprisoned in Santa Margharita.
873 Spielberg's gate: Pellico's death sentence was commuted to fifteen
years' imprisonment and he was moved to prison in Spielberg, Brunn.
896 Ninth Pius in Seventh Gregory's chair: Gregory VII (formerly
Hildebrand) became Pope in 1073. He made great claims for the worldly
power of the Church. **897 Andrea Doria's:** (1466–1560), Genoese
admiral. **903 Calvin:** (1509–64), French theologian and reformer.
904 Servetus: Miguel Serveto (1511–53), Spanish physician and theolo-
gian. He was burnt on Calvin's orders. **979 oboli:** silver Greek coins.
993 Nicae up to Trent: The Council of Nicae (AD 325); the Council of
Trent (1545–63). **1006 'Feed my lambs, Peter':** see John 21.15.
1009 Giotto: Giotto di Bondone (*c.* 1267–1337), painter and architect.
1082 Ariosto: Ludovico Ariosto (1474–1535), Italian writer.

1111 Poussin's master: presumably meaning Raphael whose style greatly influenced Nicolas Poussin (1593/4–1665), French painter active in Rome. **1112 Laura:** The addressee of many of Petrarch's love poems. **1112 Vaucluse's fount:** Petrarch lived for a time at Vaucluse in southeastern France. **1117 Charlemagne's sword:** Charlemagne was king of the Franks. He and his Paladins figure in the *Chanson de Roland*. **1124 Vespucci Amerigo:** Amerigo Vespucci (1451–1512), merchant and adventurer, from whose name 'America' is derived. He was a friend of Savonarola (see above). **1127 John Milton's Fiesole:** John Milton (1608–74), poet, author of *Paradise Lost*. He visited the European continent 1637–9. **1128 Langland's Malvern:** William Langland (1330–87), poet, author of *The Vision of Piers Plowman*, which is set in the Malvern Hills. **1129 Vallombrosa:** referring specifically to the monks who live at the abbey in Vallombrosa. **1141 St Gualbert's:** Giovanni Gualbert was founder of the Vallombrosan order. **1161 sang of Adam's paradise:** in *Paradise Lost*. **1181 Galileo:** (1564–1641), astronomer and scientist. **1190 Sorrento:** on the west coast of Italy, south of Naples. **1192 Rome's wolf:** Romulus and Remus, the brothers who founded Rome, were nursed by a she-wolf. **1195 Ovid's dreaming tales:** Ovid's *Metamorphoses* consisting of linked tales describing various shape-changes.

from Aurora Leigh

[FIRST BOOK, lines 1–64] **22 Assunta's:** the Leighs' servant. **24 scudi:** Italian coins. **53 corals to cut life upon:** teething rings made from coral. [FIRST BOOK, lines 135–215] Here Aurora gazes at a portrait of her dead mother. **86 Psyche:** Cupid, with whom Psyche was in love, had been told by Cupid not to look at him – when she did he disappeared. **87 Medusa:** mystical female associated with the Perseus story with snakes in her hair. **108 chin-bands:** devices for keeping closed the mouths of the dead. **Lazarus:** Biblical character who rose from the dead.
[FIRST BOOK, lines 385–465] Aurora describes her educational experiences with her aunt in England. **156 Articles:** the thirty-nine articles of the Church of England. **156 Tracts *against* the times:** *Tracts for the Time* (1833–) were the main writings of the Oxford movement. **157 Buonaventure's 'Prick of Love':** St Bonaventure, thirteenth-century theologian. **162 Balzac:** Honoré de Balzac (1799–1850), French novelist. His novels were often thought of as corrupting. **170 Oviedo:** Spanish historian. **172 Chimborazo:** highest peak in the Andes. **174 Lara:** Spanish town. **175 Klagenfurt:** Austrian city. **178 Johnson:** Samuel Johnson (1709–84), English writer. **182 Tophet:** hell. **183 nereids:** sea-nymphs. **186 Callarius:** French waltz.

[FIRST BOOK, lines 832–95] Aurora develops alternative ideas to those of her aunt by secretly reading her father's library.

[SECOND BOOK, lines 323–67] An early conversation between Aurora and Romney on marriage and the status of the female intellect.

[THIRD BOOK, lines 758–826] Aurora visits Marian Erle.

[FIFTH BOOK, lines 1–73] Aurora contemplates the nature of women's poetry and how it is and will be considered by men.

[SEVENTH BOOK, lines 174–227] Aurora on Marian and the position of women. **680–1:** Cervantes, Spanish author; wrote *Don Quixote*.

[SEVENTH BOOK, lines 749–94] Aurora on the nature of women's creativity. **702 Venus:** referring to the apple Venus won from Paris. **718 Antinous:** a beautiful Roman youth; more specifically a statue of Antinous in Rome.

[EIGHTH BOOK, lines 261–352] (In Italy) Romney begins by telling Aurora that he has read her work and they begin to retrace old arguments. **799 Miriam:** see Exodus 2.

[EIGHTH BOOK, lines 321–452] Marian speaking to Aurora and Romney.

[NINTH BOOK, lines 624–760] Aurora speaking to Romney. **981 inflatus:** breathing into; inspiration. **993 *in Leone*:** i.e. in Leo, the zodiacal sign.

[NINTH BOOK, lines 900–64] Begins with Romney speaking – line 964 ends the poem. **1102 inscient:** having inward knowledge, insight. **1103 visceral:** inward; deepest. **1119–20:** see Joshua 6. **1136:** see Revelations 21:5. **1144:** see Revelations 21: 19 and following.

A Curse for the Nation from *Poems Before Congress* (1860) At the time this poem was interpreted as an attack on Britain because of its attitude to Napoleon III and Italian nationalism. However the poem was written, like 'A Runaway Slave at Pilgrim's Point' (see above), at the request of the Anti-Slavery Bazaar in Boston and American slave laws are thus its primary theme. **93–4 Christ may avenge . . . the earth:** see Luke 18:7.

Mother and Poet from *Last Poems* (1862) The speaker is the female poet of the Risorgimento, Laura Savio, whose son died fighting for Italian unity. Gaeta was the last stronghold of the King of Naples, Francis II. **31 'Ancona was free!':** as part of the continuing gains for Italian forces. Ancona was beseiged in 1859. **74 Cavalli:** Giovanni Cavalli (1801–79), Italian general. **79 King Victor:** Victor Emmanuel II was proclaimed King of Italy in March 1861.